# HAUNTED PORTLAND, OREGON

# Other Books in Pelican's Haunted America Series

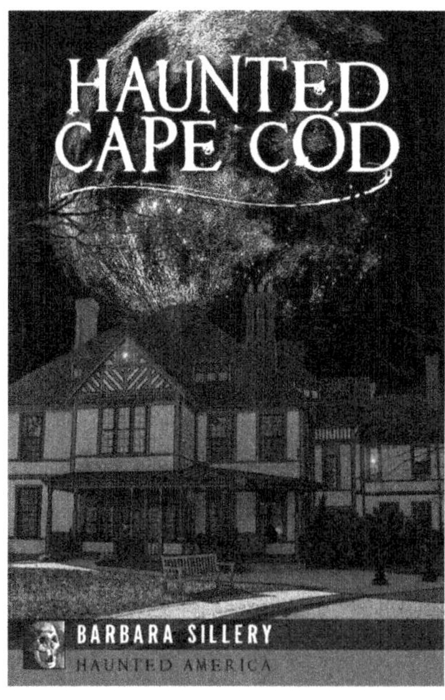

## GHOST HUNTING IN THE CITY OF ROSES

**JEFF DWYER**

**PELICAN PUBLISHING**
NEW ORLEANS

ISBN 9781455626687
Ebook ISBN 9781455626694

Printed in the United States of America
Published by Pelican Publishing
New Orleans, LA
www.pelicanpub.com

*To my sons, Sam and Michael, my stalwart companions during my travels throughout Oregon.*

# Contents

# Acknowledgments

I offer my sincere thanks to my colleagues in the field of paranormal investigation, especially Jackie Ganiy, Loyd Auerbach, Nick Groff, Zak Bagans, and Jeff Bellanger, whose inspiration, support, and encouragement I highly value.

I am also grateful to Doug Carnahan, producer and host of the *Haunted Truth* radio show, who provided me forums to discuss my ideas and experiences with colleagues at Preston Castle and Virginia City; and to my friend Zak Bagans for opportunities to appear with him on the Travel Channel shows *Ghost Adventures* and *Aftershocks*.

Many thanks to my literary agent, Sue Clark, for the support and guidance that has proved to be invaluable on countless occasions and the staff of Pelican Publishing, who, for many years, have patiently guided me through the process of producing and marketing my books.

# Introduction

In 1843, Portland was nothing more than a canoe-landing site populated by fur traders who lived in log huts or tents. A drifter from Tennessee, William Overton, and lawyer Asa Lovejoy were among the muddy settlement's residents. Both were anxious to get rich from the region's abundant natural resources, but neither owned land. Forming a partnership with 25 cents provided by Overton, the two men filed a claim on 640 acres and began clearing trees and building a road. Overton apparently grew tired of the work and moved on after selling his share of the claim to Francis Pettygrove. As a township took form, Pettygrove and Lovejoy realized the place needed a name. Each proposed to name the settlement after his hometown. Lovejoy suggested Boston while Pettygrove, who was from Maine, offered Portland. The toss of a penny settled the issue, with Pettygrove winning two of three flips of the coin.

Lovejoy and Pettygrove envisioned Portland as a great city built on the wealth of its natural resources. They also anticipated that quick prosperity would bring civilization to the Pacific Northwest. Instead, Portland went through a period of 30 years as a wild frontier town full of brothels, sailors' boardinghouses, gambling dens, and saloons that were fronts for shanghaiing ship workers. It was not until the close of the 19th century that Portland was able to rid itself of detracting monikers such as the "Forbidden City," the "Unheavenly City," "Mudville," and "Log Town" and become the "Rose City."

The 20th century finally brought the civilization envisioned by Lovejoy and Pettygrove, as prosperity turned Portland into the jewel of the Pacific Northwest. Wealth generated by great lumber mills and the shipping industry built skyscrapers in downtown Portland and fine Victorian homes in several neighborhoods, which stand today as monuments to a vision that took several decades to fulfill. All too often, the history of those decades is composed of tragic stories arising from epidemics, great fires, floods, criminal activity, and shipwrecks. These tragedies are the basis of Portland's reputation as one of the most haunted cities in the Western U.S.

Epidemics of the mid-19th century and the Spanish flu epidemic of 1918 brought tragedy to many Oregon families, ending lives at a young age and filling many pioneer cemeteries. The first recorded epidemic to hit the indigenous people of the region occurred in 1775. Fur trappers who arrived in ships brought smallpox, which decimated tribes along the Columbia River and north coast villages. Fur traders arriving in 1782 by overland routes brought a second wave of smallpox. This epidemic spread northward and was credited with wiping out half the Spokane Indian population. Smallpox struck again in 1801, leaving many Indians with pockmarked faces described by the explorers Lewis and Clark, when they arrived in 1805. Based on their report, historians believe that smallpox killed more than half of the 1800 Indian population of the western Columbia River region. Smallpox further decimated indigenous and immigrant populations in 1824 and 1853. The latter epidemic led to the opening of several pioneer cemeteries that exist today.

In 1830, malaria was imported into the Portland region. An epidemic of this disease started at Fort Vancouver and lasted four years. Accounts by officials at the fort suggest malaria nearly wiped out the entire Indian population along the lower Columbia River. The devastation caused by smallpox and malaria was so complete that after 1835, American and British immigrants to the area found few Indians. Consequently, place names that are in use today reflect the origins of the immigrants—Portland, Astoria, Salem, for example—not traditional names used by indigenous peoples such as those found in Washington state that include Seattle, Yakima, and Tacoma.

The worldwide Spanish flu epidemic of 1918 caused more deaths in Portland than most other U.S. cities. Portland suffered 505 deaths per 100,000 population compared to Indianapolis, which had only 290 deaths per 100,000. Strict quarantine ordinances were enforced and public safety laws enacted, but thousands died, overloading funeral parlors and grave-digging crews at cemeteries. In many fascinating cemeteries, such as Brainard Cemetery, Gresham Pioneer Cemetery, and the old Jones Cemetery, victims are buried in clusters. Some markers indicate that entire families, comprised of young adults and infants, occupy a single grave. Their tragic demise seems to have created spirits who have yet to let go and move on.

As with many pioneer towns, catastrophic fires destroyed some coastal settlements and portions of Portland soon after the city was founded. Fast-moving blazes often destroyed crude wooden shacks and tents, catching many residents off guard and killing them. In 1860, most of Fort Vancouver was consumed in a blaze that started in a kitchen. On August 2, 1873, Portland volunteer firefighters responded to alarms that directed them to both wealthy and poor neighborhoods. Despite their efforts, more than 20 square blocks of the city were consumed, including Chinatown and riverfront warehouses. Historical accounts do not clearly state the death toll, but it is believed that it exceeded 100 persons. Fortunately, the elegant St. Charles Hotel, hailed by the *Oregonian* as "the most magnificent structure on the northwest Pacific coast," was saved.

Large conflagrations are a thing of the past, but small fires occur often in and around Portland, creating fatalities that ultimately lead to paranormal activity. On December 9, 2010, a blaze swept through Lents Village, an apartment complex for senior citizens at 10325 SE Holgate Boulevard, Portland. Eighty residents were evacuated but one fatality occurred. On January 29, 2010, 26-year-old animal rights advocate Daniel Shaull staged a protest against Ungar Furs, a fur retailer, by dowsing himself with gasoline and igniting the vapor as he stood on the sidewalk at 1137 SW Yamhill Street. These tragedies have aroused the interest of ghost hunters, who have reported paranormal activity at the sites.

Devastating fires that resulted in several deaths have also followed airplane crashes in the greater Portland region, cities along the I-5 corridor, and coastal towns, leaving ghosts of victims that wander around towns, cities, and coastal fields. Crashes of small aircraft resulting in numerous fatalities occurred in Sherwood (2009), Hillsboro (2005, 2006), Corvallis (1995, 2000), Oregon City (1991), Salem (1990), Eugene (1977), and Portland (1999, 2005). Detailed reports of these incidents, including type of aircraft, fatalities among crew and passengers, fatalities on the ground, and location, can be found through Federal Aviation Administration websites or local newspaper accounts. The most tragic, recent airplane crashes occurred in Oregon City and Gearhart. On July 24, 2010, an experimental airplane crashed at Highway 213 and Kirk Road, in Oregon City, killing the pilot. According to witnesses, the plane was engulfed in flames as it plummeted to earth. Having nearly a minute to comprehend his impending fate, the pilot must have experienced a harrowing death. In coastal Gearhart, a small airplane crashed into a home on August 6, 2008, creating an intense fire that killed five people.

The worst commercial disaster in Portland occurred December 28, 1978, when a United Airlines DC-8 (N8082U) with 181 passengers and crew ran out of fuel and crashed into a residential area between East Burnside Street and NE 160th Avenue. Miraculously, only 10 persons were killed on impact, while 24 were seriously injured. The neighborhood is densely populated but no houses currently stand at the site of the crash. The ground is covered with a stand of trees that surrounds a parking area.

Portland and several nearby communities have endured criminal activity and social injustice that have led to hauntings and legends of ghosts. The misdeeds of several 19th-century outlaws produced many used, abused, confused, and forlorn spirits who stay with us long after their death. The souls of these victims may still seek lost dreams while they remain attached to what little they gained during their difficult lives. Many ghosts who harbor deep resentment, pain, or a desire to complete their unfinished business still roam courthouses, hotels, theatres, modern buildings, cemeteries, and other public places throughout the region.

Like most metropolitan areas in the U.S., Portland has had several crime sprees linked to organized crime and illegal drugs. Deaths of victims, perpetrators, and occasionally police officers have left intense paranormal activity at several locations around the city. In the 19th century, gang-related crime was rampant, starting in 1836 with the murder of two women. Gang activity was so extreme that a police force was created in 1844. Riots in 1863 were linked to the Civil War and, in 1870 and 1874, labor unrest. These riots led to several deaths and improvements in the police force.

The greatest criminal activity of the 19th century was created by the shanghai industry. Starting in 1850, unscrupulous saloon operators discovered they could make a lot of money by kidnapping inebriated men and delivering them to waiting ships, where they were pressed into service by captains desperate for a crew. The industry quickly became sophisticated, with trapdoors in the floors of saloons, underground holding areas, and a complex network of tunnels beneath the city's streets that enabled abductors to deliver their captives to the waterfront. Business was so brisk that Portland was known as one of the most dangerous ports in the world and given the moniker "Forbidden City of the West." Many men who fell through trapdoors died upon impact on the concrete floors below. Others died from beatings or illnesses aggravated by their alcoholism. It is unknown how many men died in Portland's famous underground city, but the tunnels are world-renowned for paranormal activity and exciting tours. In the 1920s and 1930s, the tunnels were expanded, reaching into Chinatown and downtown Portland, and became venues for illegal businesses such as gambling, bootlegging, and prostitution. Tours of the tunnels feature holding cells, a former opium den, cells for breaking the will of young women, trapdoors, and other artifacts.

In the 1980s and early 1990s, Portland's violent-crime rate soared due to a crack cocaine epidemic. Several murders were linked to this illegal trade, while numerous drug users were found dead on city streets or in hotels and apartment houses. By 1993, law enforcement and other measures ended the epidemic and the crime rate dropped sharply. In 2005, the city achieved its lowest crime rate since the late 19th century. Extensive surveillance of high-crime areas led to a reduction in homicides to less than 500 in 2007 and 466 in 2009. This still leaves hundreds of crime scenes that have attracted the attention of paranormal investigators, including the Bethany triple-murder site.

On November 2, 2006, Ricardo Serrano entered a house at 2902 NW Telshire Terrace, in Beaverton, and shot to death three occupants. Two of the victims were children. This horrific crime created intense imprints or residuals that have been detected by sensitive psychics standing in front of the house.

An event that seems to have triggered a tragic series of shootings in public places took place at Clackamas Town Center mall on December 11, 2012. Twenty-two-year-old Jacob Tyler Roberts entered the mall with an AR-15 assault rifle and opened fire on shoppers and employees. After seriously wounding a 15-year-old girl and killing two others, Roberts ended the horrific event by killing himself.

Paranormal investigators who are interested in taking a forensic approach to ghost hunting may want to visit crime scenes listed in reports of serial killers who committed crimes in the Portland region. Detailed information about Randall Woodfield, known as the I-5 killer, and the killing spree perpetrated by Jerry Brudos may be found by searching the Internet.

Historical records dating from the 19th century indicate several maritime disasters on the Columbia and Willamette Rivers. On April 8, 1854, the steamship *Gazelle* suffered a boiler explosion while approaching the docks near Oregon

City. Twenty-four passengers and crew were killed, their body parts scattered all over the waterfront. Among the victims were local businessmen Crawford Dobbins and D. P. Fuller, who were among the first to be interred in the new Lone Fir Cemetery in central Portland.

Situated at the confluence of two great rivers, the Columbia and Willamette, Portland has endured several floods, some of which resulted in many fatalities and the 19th-century nickname "Mudville." The geology of the Pleistocene era reveals that some of the world's greatest known floods occurred in the Portland area. In the early 19th century, numerous floods were recorded by Hudson's Bay Company officials at Fort Vancouver and others who explored the Columbia River gorge. Until recently, floods were commonplace, resulting from heavy rainfall and melting snowfields to the east. In 1890, the Columbia River overflowed its banks, washing away several houseboats, small boats, barges, docks, and other waterfront facilities. The unofficial death toll exceeded 30. In June of 1894, the Willamette River rose more than 30 feet above it banks, flooding the entire business district of Portland, including the infamous shanghai tunnels. Waters receded so slowly that sewage was spread through the city, contaminating wells, cisterns, and other water supplies. After several deaths, the city issued warnings to all citizens advising them to boil drinking water, use disinfectants, and consider spending the summer in the mountains or at the coast.

The greatest flood to hit the city in modern times occurred on May 30, 1948. The Vanport City neighborhood, occupied by more than 20,000 people, mostly African American shipyard workers, was virtually destroyed when a 200-foot-long dike collapsed. Columbia River waters inundated the enclave, creating a disaster that rivals the flooding of New Orleans after Hurricane Katrina. The official death toll was only 15, but unofficial accounts place the numbers much higher. The worst flood on the Willamette River in the modern era occurred from December 18, 1964, to January 7, 1965. Killing 17 people and causing hundreds of millions of dollars in damage, floodwaters covered 152,789 acres and destroyed countless businesses and homes. As recently as 1996, the Willamette and Columbia Rivers continued their winter rampages, inundating several communities but failing to breach the seawall in downtown Portland. Deaths occurred from drowning, electrocution, and infection.

Situated on the Pacific Rim, Portland often experienced earthquakes. Lewis and Clark noted Indian reports of great movements of the earth that occurred decades before their arrival in 1805. On November 23, 1873, an earthquake struck that shook buildings as far away as San Francisco. The Richter scale was not in use at that time, but eyewitness accounts mention the collapse of several chimneys and brick buildings that trapped and killed residents. Large earthquakes occurred in 1877, 1896, 1913, and 1915. The great San Francisco earthquake of April 19, 1906, damaged buildings in Portland. More recently, a series of earthquakes struck Oregon between May 26 and June 11, 1968. In 1993, a 6.0 earthquake caused millions of dollars in damage and killed three people.

All of these tragic events add to the region's ghost legacy and have left powerful emotional imprints created by spirits of the dearly departed who felt a need to stay on. A common factor is the loss of life by a sudden, violent event, often at a young age. Unfortunate crewmembers of the many ships sunk off the treacherous coast, shanghaied sailors, firefighters, passengers in airplanes, and indigenous people who died of imported diseases or from skirmishes with settlers all passed with great emotional anguish, leaving their souls with an inextinguishable desire to achieve their life's objectives, or with a sense of obligation to offer protection to a particular place or person.

Some ghosts remain on the earthly plane for revenge or to provide guidance for someone still alive. Many of those who came to Oregon for the fur trade, free land, or employment in the logging and shipping industries were caught up in their dreams but met only with frustration and failure before dying alone and in poverty. Their restless spirits still roam the old neighborhoods of Portland.

## ABOUT THIS BOOK

Chapter 1 of this book will help you, the ghost hunter, to research and organize your own ghost hunt at locations within the region. Chapters 2 through 5 describe several locations at which ghostly activity has been reported in the greater Portland area and cities along the I-5, which conveys travelers to and from Portland. Unlike other collections of ghost stories and descriptions of haunted places, this book emphasizes access. Private homes and other buildings not open to visitors are not included. Addresses of each haunted site are provided along with other information to assist you in finding and entering the location. Appendixes offer recommended reading and list movies that were filmed in the Portland area in order to introduce you to the culture and the region.

## WHAT IS A GHOST?

A ghost is some aspect of the personality, spirit, consciousness, energy, mind, intelligence, or soul that remains after the body dies. When any these are detected by the living—through sight, sound, odor, tactile sensations, or movement of objects—we may consider the experience to be a paranormal encounter. The encounter may be said to be "ghostly" if there is intelligent interaction with a witness or the environment. This includes interaction by touching, speaking, gestures, facial expressions, movement of objects, and sounds such as tapping in response to questions. It also includes creation of sounds or other electronic analogs on audio recorders and other instrumentation.

The essential criterion for concluding that a ghostly encounter has occurred is intelligent interaction with a living person or the environment. If this strict criterion cannot be met, it is likely that the experience involves something other than a ghost. I've estimated that more than 80 percent of paranormal experiences have nothing to do with a ghost.

The *intelligent* events that may differentiate ghosts from other paranormal activity include specific interaction with the living, performance of a purposeful activity, or a response to ongoing changes in the environment. Ghosts may speak to the living to warn of an unforeseen accident or disaster, to give advice, or to express their love, anger, remorse, or disappointment. They may also try to complete some project or duty they failed to finish before death. Some ghosts try to move furniture, room decorations, or the like to suit their preferences.

Occasionally, paranormal activity is bizarre and frightening, or it appears to be dangerous. Witnesses may see objects fly about, hear ominous sounds, or experience accidents. This kind of activity is sometimes attributed to a "poltergeist" or noisy ghost. Most authorities believe that a living person, not the dead, causes these manifestations. Generally, a person under great emotional stress releases psychic energy that creates subtle or spectacular changes in the environment. Noises commonly associated with a poltergeist include tapping on walls or ceilings, heavy footsteps, shattering glass, ringing telephones, and running water. Objects may move about on tables or floors or fly across a room. Furniture may spin or tip over. Dangerous objects, such as knives, hammers, or pens, may hit people. These poltergeist events may last a few days, a year, or more. Discovery and removal of the emotionally unstable, living person often stops the poltergeist.

Always be aware that many other paranormal phenomena can appear to be ghostly manifestations. Reference to the essential criterion can help you determine if you are dealing with an imprint or other paranormal phenomenon. Keep in mind that ghostly activity is real time; the ghost is present. Imprint phenomena represent something from the past. By definition, imprints lack intelligent interaction with the witness or the environment and occur without the consciousness of a dead person.

## HOW DOES A GHOST MANIFEST ITSELF?

The process by which a ghost manifests itself is not

completely understood, but there are many useful theories that help us understand ghostly behavior.

Ghosts interact with our environment in a variety of ways that may have something to do with the strength of their personality and desire to communicate in the context of confusion resulting from their transformation by death. The talents or skills they possessed in life, their personal objectives, or frustrations arising from the end of life may underlie their efforts in getting our attention. A sudden, traumatic death, strong ties to surviving loved ones or a particular place, unfinished business, strong emotions such as hatred and anger, or a desire for revenge may also trigger ghostly activity.

A ghost may create a change in the environment. Movement of objects such as books, a pipe, eyeglasses, tools, weapons, doorknobs, bedding, etc., that cannot be attributed to normal or natural processes often indicates the presence of a ghost. Some ghosts have been known to rearrange furniture or room decorations to suit their preferences. If new objects are placed in a ghost's favorite room, they may be found moved outside the room, broken, or hidden in another location. Common ghostly activities are movement of a rocking chair, turning of doorknobs, activation of light switches and electronic equipment such as TVs, and disheveling bedding. Ghosts like to knock over stacks of cards or coins, scatter matchsticks, and move your keys. It appears easy for many to manipulate light switches and TV remotes, open and close windows and doors, or push chairs around. Some ghosts have the power to throw objects, pull pictures from walls, or move heavy items. As a rule, ghosts cannot tolerate disturbances within the place they haunt. If you tilt a wall-mounted picture, the ghost will set it straight. Obstacles placed in the ghost's path may be pushed aside.

Some ghosts create odors, particularly those associated with their habits, such as cigar smoke or signature perfumes. Many reports from credible witnesses mention the odors of tobacco, oranges, and hemp as most common.

Ghosts can also create impressions that the physical qualities of an environment have changed when, in fact, no physical transformation has occurred. Ice-cold breezes and unexplained gusts of wind are often the first signs that a ghost is present. Moving or stationary cold spots, with temperatures several degrees below surrounding areas, have been detected. Temperature changes sometimes occur with a feeling that the atmosphere has thickened, as if the room was suddenly filled with unseen people.

In searching for ghosts, some people use devices that detect changes in magnetic, electrical, or radio fields. However, detected changes may be subject to error, interference by other electrical devices, or misinterpretation. Measurements indicating the presence of a ghost may be difficult to capture on a permanent record.

Ghosts may create images such as luminous fogs, balls of light called "orbs," streaks of light, or the partial outline of body parts on still cameras (film or digital) and video recorders. In the 19th century, this was called spirit photography. Captured images are sometimes spectacular, but modern digital photographs are easily edited, making it difficult to produce convincing proof of ghostly activity.

The experience of seeing humanoid images is the prized objective of most ghost hunters, but it is rare. When such images are seen, they are often partial, revealing only a head and torso with an arm or two. Feet are seldom seen. Full-body apparitions are extremely rare. Some ghost hunters have seen ethereal, fully transparent forms that are barely discernible. Others report seeing ghosts who appear as solid as a living being.

## WHY DO GHOSTS REMAIN AT A PARTICULAR PLACE?

Ghosts remain in a particular place because they are emotionally attached to a room, a building, or special surroundings that profoundly affected them during their lives or to activities or events that played a role in their death. A prime example is the haunted house inhabited by the ghost of a man who hung himself in the master bedroom because his wife left him. It is widely believed that death and sudden transition from the physical world confuses a ghost. He or she remains in familiar or emotionally stabilizing surroundings to ease the strain. A place-bound ghost is most likely to occur when a violent death occurred with great emotional anguish. Ghosts may linger in a house, barn, cemetery, factory, or store waiting for a loved one or anyone familiar who might help them deal with their new level of existence. Some ghosts wander through buildings or forests, on bridges, or alongside particular sections of roads. Some await enemies, seeking revenge. Others await a friend for a chance to resolve their guilt.

There seems to be a close association between aspects of the entity's life and the modalities it uses to manifest itself on our plane of existence. These include places and objects related to sudden, traumatic death; strong ties to surviving loved ones or a particular place; unfinished business; strong emotions such as hatred and anger; or a desire for revenge.

There may be other reasons, but these motivations explain most spirit activity. Most spirits are place-bound rather than people-bound. That is, they are attached to, or drawn to, a particular place such as a house, office, airplane, boat, or movie theatre. This contention is supported by the idea that most ghosts do not travel. For example, a person who feels that his house is haunted rarely reports the same ghostly activity at his workplace, gym, grocery store, etc. This suggests that the ghost has no interest in following the living person to various locations because it is *attached* to a particular place. The ghost may be interested in living persons, but the primary basis of the haunting is a *place*.

## UNDER WHAT CONDITIONS IS A SIGHTING MOST LIKELY?

Although ghosts may appear at any time, a sighting may occur on special holidays, anniversaries, birthdays, or during historic periods (July 4, December 7, September 11), or calendar periods pertaining to the personal history of the ghost. Halloween is reputed to be a favorite night for many apparitions, while others seem to prefer their own special day or night, on a weekly or monthly cycle.

Night is a traditional time for ghost activity, yet experienced ghost hunters know that sightings may occur at any time. Despite the tradition of overnight investigations presented in many paranormal TV shows, there seems to be no consistent affinity of ghosts for darkness, but they seldom appear when artificial light is bright. Perhaps this is why ghosts shy away from camera crews and their array of lights. Ghosts seem to prefer peace and quiet, although some of them have been reported to make incessant, loud sounds. Even a small group of ghost hunters may make too much noise to facilitate a sighting. For this reason, it is recommended that you limit your group to four persons and oral communication be kept to a minimum.

## IS GHOST HUNTING DANGEROUS?

Ghost hunting can be hazardous, but reports of injuries inflicted by ghosts are rare and their veracity suspect. Movies and children's ghost stories have created a widespread notion that ghosts may harm the living or even cause the death of persons they dislike. In 2006, a popular television program showed a fascinating video of a ghost hunter being struck down by his camera equipment. The man's heavy equipment moved suddenly from a position at his waist and struck him on the side of the face. Video of this event was interpreted as evidence of a ghost attack but no apparition or light anomaly was visible. Decades ago, the Abbot of Trondheim ghost was reputed to have attacked some people, but circumstances and precipitating events are unclear.

Many authorities believe that rare attacks by ghosts are a matter of mistaken identity, i.e., the ghost misidentified a living person as a figure the ghost knew during his life. It is possible that encounters that appear to be attacks may be nothing more than clumsy efforts by a ghost to achieve recognition. Witnesses of ghost appearances have found themselves in the middle of gunfights, major military battles, and other violent events yet sustained not the slightest injury.

Persons who claim to have been injured by a ghost have, in most cases, precipitated the injury themselves through their own ignorance or fear. Ghost hunters often carry out investigations in the dark or subdued light and may encounter environmental hazards that lead to injury. Fear may trigger an attempt to race from a haunted site, exposing the ghost hunter to injury by tripping over unseen objects or making contact with broken glass, low-hanging tree limbs, exposed wiring, or weakened floorboards, stairways, or doorways.

You, the ghost hunter, will be safe if you keep a wary eye and a calm attitude and set aside tendencies to fear the ghost or the circumstances of its appearance. Safety may be enhanced if you visit a haunted location while it is well illuminated, during daylight hours for instance. Potential hazards in the environment can be identified and, perhaps, cleared or marked with light-reflecting tape.

Most authorities agree that ghosts do not travel. Ghosts will not follow you home, take up residence in your car, or attempt to occupy your body. They are held in a time and space by deep emotional ties to an event or place. Ghosts have been observed on airplanes, trains, buses, and ships; however, it is unlikely that the destination interests them. Something about the journey, some event such as a plane crash or train wreck, accounts for their appearance as travelers. In some cases, it is the conveyance that ties the ghost to the physical plane. A vintage World War II B-17 bomber may be haunted by the ghost of a man who piloted that type of aircraft in the 1940s. A ship, such as the *Queen Mary* in Long Beach, California, may be an irresistible attraction for the ghost of a sailor who once worked on passenger liners.

## IMPRINTS

The vast majority of paranormal experiences involve imprint phenomena. Psychics who search for ghosts need to understand this phenomenon, because it can easily be confused with a ghost. If intelligent interaction has not been demonstrated, we must conclude that we are dealing with something that is not ghostly and we may call it an "imprint phenomenon." If the principal feature of this phenomenon is an inanimate object, it is called a "phantom." If it is comprised of a humanoid apparition or vocalization, we may call it an "apparition," being careful to add whenever possible the distinction that it is not ghostly.

Imprints and ghostly manifestations may appear similar. They have common features in terms of what witnesses see, feel, or smell, but an imprint may occur without the presence of a spiritual entity or the consciousness of a dead person. People have reported seeing pale, transparent images of the deceased walking in hallways, climbing stairs, sitting in rocking chairs, or sitting in airplanes, trains, buses, and even restaurants. Some have been observed sleeping in beds, hanging by ropes from trees, or walking through walls. Most commonly, a partial apparition is seen, but witnesses have reported seeing entire armies engaged in battle. Unlike ghosts, hauntings do not display intelligent action with respect to the location—they do not manipulate your computer—and they do not interact with the living.

Imprints may be environmental recordings of something that happened at a location as a result of the repetition of intense emotion. As such, they tend to be associated with a specific place or object, not a particular person. Ghostly figures tend to perform some kind of repetitive task or activity. Sometimes the haunting is so repetitive that witnesses feel as though they are watching a video loop that plays the same brief scene over and over. A good example is that of a deceased grandmother who makes appearances seated in her favorite rocking chair. She rocks for a few seconds and then disappears, only to reappear later performing the same action. If the chair does not move and the ghostly image appears oblivious to witnesses or changes in the local environment, this is an imprint, not a ghost.

## TYPES OF IMPRINTS

Imprints may create a variety of experiences in six primary categories:

1. **Olfactory (clairsentient):** This means the perception of odors or fragrances, which may include perfume, flowers, animal odors, fruit such as oranges, hemp, tobacco, rotting meat, sour milk, or smoke.

2. **Auditory (clairaudient):** This refers to sounds such as vocalizations, including spoken words, humming, whistling, yawning, and sobbing; and non-vocalizations such as musical instruments, footsteps, gunshots, horse's hooves, slamming doors, and breaking glass. These sounds may be heard normally, psychically, or only through recording equipment.

3. **Visual (clairvoyant):** These may be amorphous shapes, humanoid shadows, partial apparitions, or full-bodied apparitions. They may be seen by one witness but not another, suggesting a psychic process or individual differences in sensitivity.

4. **Photographic:** This means paranormal images (those lacking a "normal" explanation) not seen with the eyes but found in still pictures or video, film or digital, including orbs, streaks of light, unexplained shadows, or humanoid shapes.

5. **Tactile (clairsentient):** In some instances, energy emanates from imprints that may create bizarre impressions of a crowded space or the close presence of an unseen being. Other perceptions include thickened air and even cold spots. It is important to note that imprints do not create the kind of tactile experiences ghosts may produce. Ghosts may leave scratch marks, a handprint, and bruises. Imprints don't leave physical evidence of contact.

**6. Emotional (empathic):** Pleasant and unpleasant emotions may be imprinted on the environment or an object and perceived by a sensitive person. Emotions may be specific and linked to a particular place or item such as weapons, jewelry, musical instruments, coins and medallions, and doorknobs.

## CHARACTERISTICS OF IMPRINTS

It is important to understand that imprints are the result of something that happened in the past. As such, they are the foundation of retrocognition. When we detect an imprint, we experience an odor, emotion, sound, or image that was an element of a past event. This distinction becomes especially important when we investigate crime scenes. Imprints can reveal the movement of a victim and perpetrator, weapons and other objects involved in the crime, and other elements that may not be discovered in a police investigation. A good example of the latter is the familiarity of the victim with the perpetrator.

Imprints can also provide valuable clues that lead to an encounter with a ghost. Called "hot spots" by some psychics, intense imprints can be anchoring points that attach ghosts to a particular place.

Olfactory perceptions may range from the engaging fragrance of expensive perfume to the horrible stench of rotted meat. It is often useful to identify the fragrance, such as magnolia or Chanel No. 5 perfume. Linked with background research, this may indicate that a former female occupant of a house loved magnolias or used Chanel perfume. This link can lead to identification of the person whose emotional experience created the imprint. Offensive odors could be the result of illness that preceded death or the process of decomposition that occurred when a dead body was left undiscovered for a long time.

Auditory imprints comprise the majority of non-ghostly

paranormal experiences. Sensitive psychics may mentally "hear" a variety of sounds, such as human vocalizations, musical instruments, gunshots, footsteps, the movement of horse-drawn carriages, slamming doors, etc. Auditory imprints are readily captured on recording devices, too. Thousands of high-quality recordings known as electronic voice phenomena (EVP) and electronic audio phenomena (EAP) may be found on the Internet.

The most exciting imprint phenomenon is the sighting of a humanoid apparition. Apparitions may appear as dark shadows, figures composed of white smoke or fog, transparent partial body parts, transparent whole-body figures, and lifelike bodies. The ability to perceive imprint apparitions varies greatly among people. The most ardent ghost hunter may never see one, while a casual visitor to a historic site may spot several.

## HOT SPOTS FOR GHOSTLY ACTIVITY

Numerous sites of disasters, criminal activity, suicides, devastating fires, and other tragic events abound in Portland, providing hundreds of opportunities for ghost hunting. You may visit the locations described in chapters 2-5 to experience ghostly activity discovered by others or discover a hot spot to research and initiate your own original ghost investigation.

Astute ghost hunters often search historical maps, drawings, and other documents to find the sites of military conflicts, buildings that no longer exist, or sites of tragic events now occupied by modern structures. For example, maps and drawings found online or displayed in museums, such as Fort Vancouver, the Oregon Maritime Museum, the Oregon History Museum, and the Pearson Air Museum in nearby Vancouver, Washington, or at historic locations such as the Pittock Mansion, may be a good place to start.

People who died in natural or maritime disasters or train or stagecoach robberies, of epidemics, or from infections that ensued after minor injuries, and those displaced by other tragic events such as fires, may remain with us as active ghosts. In Portland, ghosts haunt the site of their unmarked graves, favorite bars or restaurants, workplaces, mysterious tunnels, shipwrecks, or cherished homes.

Historic homes of pioneers and early residents are often the focal point for successful ghost investigations. These places typically offer a well-researched history, authentic artifacts, personal belongings of former occupants, and easy accessibility. Among the most famous historic homes in the Portland region, now open as restaurants, inns, or museums, are the 1911-vintage White House, former home of lumber baron Robert Lytle; the Pittock Mansion (1909), center of a political scandal involving one of its owners, Will H. Daly; the McLoughlin House (1846), home of Fort Vancouver manager Dr. John McLoughlin; the Barclay House (1850), home of Fort Vancouver physician Forbes Barclay; the Ermatinger House (1845), built by Francis Ermatinger and site of the famous coin toss in 1845 that gave Portland its name; the George C. Marshall House (1889), home of the famous general and Nobel Peace Prize winner; the Ulysses S. Grant House (1846), used by the general before the Civil War; and the Stevens-Crawford House (1907), home of Mary E. Crawford and Harley Stevens.

Fascinating histories and ghostly atmospheres may also be found in historic commercial buildings and homes that are now modern businesses, such as the legendary White Eagle Café, the Crow Bar (housed in Fort Vancouver's Grant House), Old Town Pizza, Commodore Grocery, the White House restaurant, Yellow Brick Road Antiques store, and the Bagdad Theater.

Portland and nearby cities have established historic districts and other venues that have attracted the attention of professional and amateur ghost hunters. These include the preserved and restored structures of downtown Portland, the former warehouse and industrial area now known as the Pearl District, Old Town Chinatown, the trendy subcultural-oriented Hawthorne District, and Alameda Ridge, which contains some of the oldest homes in the region.

Travelers on I-5 may want to visit Eugene's South University Historic District and the Blair Historic District anchored by Sam Bond's Garage. In Salem, horse-drawn carriages and streetcars preserve the historic atmosphere of the 19th century.

Fort Vancouver offers ghost hunters opportunities to visit some of the most historic structures in the Portland region. Founded in 1824, the rustic fort was nearly destroyed in 1866 by a major fire. It was quickly rebuilt with a Victorian architectural motif modified to serve military needs. Among the buildings targeted for paranormal investigation by local ghost hunters are the houses of Officers Row, including the Grant House (now a restaurant), the McLoughlin House, the Barclay House, the George C. Marshall House, and the General O. O. Howard House; the former post hospital; and the 1919-vintage Red Cross building.

Many churches established in the 19th and early 20th centuries exist throughout the Portland area, some standing next to graveyards that contain pioneers and notable historic figures. The cornerstone of the Victorian-style Calvary Presbyterian Church, known as "the Old Church," was laid on September 11, 1882. Thought to be "too far out in the country" by its earliest members, it is located in what is downtown Portland today. The Old Church, cited as one of the most beautiful buildings in the Pacific Northwest, no longer serves a congregation. It is currently used as a social venue for weddings, lectures, concerts, plays, and meetings. The historic character and spooky atmosphere of the Old Church are accented by its amazing architectural features.

Built in a Gothic Revival style, the Zion Lutheran Church was opened in 1890. A newer church now occupies the site, but architectural remnants remain. The newer church was dedicated in 1950, and several emotional events have occurred in the sanctuary and narthex that have created residual paranormal imprints. The Venetian Gothic-style First Congregational Church on Park Avenue in Portland opened in 1895. Massive stone arches, huge stained-glass windows, brick construction, and the off-center tower give the place a beautiful, eerie appearance. In the Portland suburb of

Milwaukie, the Oaks Pioneer Church has been serving its congregation since 1865. The old church has been moved three times, once on a river barge, and underwent major renovations in 1869, 1883, and 1928.

These regionally important churches are accessible to the general public, and ghost hunters, as places of historical interest while most continue to offer worship services.

Ghost hunters who have an interest in old churches should visit nearby Salem, where 14 historic churches may be found. Of particular interest are St. Joseph Catholic Church (1853), First Baptist Church (1859), and First United Methodist Church (1878). Farther south, along the I-5 corridor, the First Christian Church of Eugene (1911) has a massive dome and huge stained-glass windows that create a sacred ambience, but spirits are also attached to the place.

Across the boulevard from Fort Vancouver, the stately French-Carpenter Gothic-style Providence Academy building was opened in 1874 as a young ladies' school. The chapel was dedicated as a religious center in 1883. Once considered the official chapel of Fort Vancouver, the place served as a venue for funerals and memorial services.

Several historic cemeteries in the Portland region provide plenty of opportunities to discover fascinating histories of early residents and experience a paranormal encounter. Many of them date from the mid-19th century and include interesting architecture, intriguing epitaphs, and overgrown foliage that create a spooky atmosphere. These cities of the dead include unusual tombs, peculiar statuary, and unmarked mass graves. Here you will find Portland's pioneers, politicians, prostitutes, civic leaders, cultural icons, and a few criminals.

Established during the homesteading period of 1850 to 1870, many of the metropolitan region's 14 pioneer graveyards are well known by local ghost hunters as good places to experience paranormal phenomena. The oldest graveyards are Powell Grove Cemetery, containing headstones with death dates from 1837, and Lone Fir Cemetery, which was opened in 1846. The Columbian Cemetery contains graves of veterans of the Civil War and every subsequent war, including those in Iraq and Afghanistan. Ghost hunters fascinated by military history should visit the Grand Army of the Republic Cemetery in Southwest Portland. Douglass Cemetery contains the grave of its founder, John Douglass, who fought in the War of 1812, traveled west on the Oregon Trail, and subsequently became a prominent Portland shipbuilder.

A few miles from downtown Portland, Gresham Pioneer Cemetery began burials in 1859, offering a final resting place to loggers and train operators who died in the many disasters that occurred in the region's forests. It also contains the remains of locals who served as Union soldiers, sailors, and marines in the Civil War.

Asylums, prisons, and farms for the indigent almost always opened burial grounds for residents who died while detained or incarcerated. Often, these burial grounds contain unmarked or desecrated graves, which retain spirits at the site. The Multnomah County Poor Farm Cemetery is one of those burial sites that have been the target of ghost hunters who seek the spirits of people who were condemned to misery and hopelessness in life only to suffer the indignity of a disturbed or ignominious grave after death. Located southeast of Mount Calvary Cemetery, the poor-farm graves include a colony of lepers and countless others who were sick, poor, or mentally ill.

Despite its location across the Columbia River in the state of Washington, the city of Vancouver has close geographic, historic, and cultural ties with Portland. The Old City Cemetery in Vancouver contains the remains of some of Portland's pioneers and offers the region's ghost hunters fascinating histories of colorful figures and a few ghosts. The earliest burials were made within the present limits of Vancouver Barracks. In the 1860s, another cemetery was opened near the west boundary of the Post, across Reserve Street from the Academy. As Fort Vancouver and the surrounding community grew, many graves from these early sites were moved. In 1867, the city purchased 10 acres of John Maney's Land Claim and began relocating graves from earlier sites. Despite care, many headstones were misplaced and some were set over the wrong graves. This often leads to ghostly activity. In March of 2011, paranormal activity increased after vandals pushed over 44 monuments along the southwest corner of the cemetery.

Founded in 1882, River View Cemetery contains some peculiar monuments that may have enticed spirits to stay behind in our physical world. Simon Benson, Portland's wealthiest lumberman in 1907, is buried in Section 8. His grave marker is a simple granite block, but monuments to Benson's civic pride remain all over downtown Portland in the form of drinking fountains known as Benson Bubblers. Minnie Merchant Smith's grave is topped with a marble angel that casts fascinating shadows around the burial site. One of the most visited graves in the cemetery is that of frontier gunfighter and lawman Virgil Earp. Brother of famed lawman Wyatt Earp, Virgil died in 1905 in Nevada, but his body was brought to Portland by his daughter, Janie Law.

The most fascinating and spiritually active graveyard in the Portland region may be Lone Fir Cemetery. Founded in 1846 as a burial ground for the Stephens family, the place became a community cemetery in 1854 to accommodate victims of a tragic steamboat explosion on the Willamette River. It covers 30 acres with more than 25,000 graves. Lone Fir Cemetery staff members conduct monthly tours, which reveal fascinating histories and clues to paranormal activity that occurs there. Visitors have experienced paranormal activity at several sites, including Dr. Hawthorne's plot, which contains the remains of 132 patients from his insane asylum, and Block 14, which contains an unknown number of bodies in unmarked graves.

Most county websites list pioneer cemeteries and offer links to local organizations that care for the graves and grounds. The best way to see these cemeteries, and learn fascinating histories of those entombed, is to tour them with a knowledgeable guide. Some of these places are too spooky and possibly unsafe after dark unless you are accompanied by people who can ensure a pleasant visit.

## THREE SIMPLE RULES

Three simple rules apply for successful ghost hunting. The first is to be patient. Ghosts are everywhere, but contact may require a considerable investment of time. Second, respect the boundaries of private property and the rights of property owners to restrict or deny access to places you may wish to investigate. The third rule is to have fun. Ghost hunting can be a fascinating and exciting experience. You may report your ghost-hunting experiences or suggest hot spots for ghost hunting to the author via e-mail at jeffhdwyer@yahoo.com. Visit the author's website at www.jeffdwyer.com.

## CHAPTER 1

# How to Hunt Ghosts

You may want to visit recognized haunted sites, listed in chapters 2 through 5, using some of the ghost-hunting techniques described in this chapter or search for a new haunted site in the Portland area. Your search for a ghost, or exploration of a haunted place, starts with research. Summaries of obscure and esoteric material about possible haunted sites are available from museums, local historical societies, and bookstores. Brochures and booklets, sold at historical sites under the Oregon State Parks system, can be good resources too.

By touring a haunted venue, you will have opportunities to speak with guides and docents who may be able to provide you with anecdotes about the dearly departed or share ghost stories you can't find in published material. Guided tours of historical sites such as the famous Shanghai Tunnels in Portland; old neighborhoods in Eugene, Salem, Oregon City, and Troutdale; the historic grounds of Fort Vancouver; or old churches and pioneer graveyards are good places to begin your research. Tours can help you develop a feel for places within a building where ghosts might be sighted or an appreciation of relevant history.

A visit to a local graveyard is also useful in identifying possible ghosts. Often you can find headstones that indicate the person entombed died of suicide, criminal activity, local disaster, or such. Some epitaphs may indicate that the deceased was survived by a spouse and children or died far from home. Grave markers that have been desecrated or damaged by weather, vegetation, erosion, or earthquakes are good places to look for paranormal phenomena.

## TWO BASIC METHODS FOR FINDING GHOSTS

If your visit is spontaneous or initiated with little or no time for preparation and research, use simple methods and minimal instrumentation in your efforts to experience ghosts and capture evidence of their manifestation. An audio recorder, still or video camera, dowsing rods, and a few trigger objects may be more than sufficient and are easily transported in a backpack or large purse.

If you plan a lengthy, formal investigation during a period of special access, you may want to include more specialized instrumentation. Some ghost hunters will feel competent with a collection of cameras, electromagnetic field detectors, digital thermometers, data recorders, and other high-tech gadgets. These ghost hunters prefer to use the Technical Method.

Others may discover they have an emotional affinity for a particular historic site, a surprising fascination with an event associated with a haunting, or empathy for a deceased person. These ghost hunters may have success with the Psychic Method.

Another consideration is the ghost hunter's goal. Some desire scientific evidence of ghostly presence while others simply want to experience paranormal activity. This chapter will help you select equipment and methodologies that will enhance your experience.

## THE TECHNICAL METHOD

Ghost hunters who favor the Technical Method often use an array of detection and recording devices that cover a wide range of the electromagnetic spectrum. Some technical methods of ghost hunting can be complicated and expensive and require skilled people to operate the devices. Ghost hunters who want to use the Technical Method yet keep their investigations simple and inexpensive may get satisfying results with common audio and video recording devices and other low-tech approaches.

**Equipment Preparation**

A few days before your ghost hunt, clear audio and image media of previous recordings. Test your batteries and bring new backup batteries and freshly charged power packs to the investigation site. You should have two types of flashlights: a broad-beam light for moving around a site and a penlight-type flashlight for narrow-field illumination. A red lens will help you avoid disruption of your night-adapted vision.

**Still-Photography Techniques**

Many photographic techniques and default digital camera settings that work well under normal conditions are inadequate for ghost hunts. If you use digital photographic methods, practice taking pictures under conditions of low ambient light, with and without artificial lighting. Some ghost hunters use infrared photography. Because digital cameras are inherently sensitive to infrared light, minor adjustments allow users to take pictures that may reveal entities that would not be seen with conventional photographic techniques. Filters may be purchased that block visible light while admitting infrared light. Many cameras also have features that enable automatic exposures at specific intervals, e.g., once every minute. This allows a hands-off remote image record to be made. Your equipment should also include a stable, lightweight tripod.

While every ghost hunter armed with a camera wishes to capture the full-bodied image of a ghost, most have to settle for light anomalies. These may be amorphous, luminescent clouds or narrow streaks of light resembling a shooting star. The light anomaly most frequently captured with digital photography is the orb. An orb is a symmetrical, white disk that appears most often in digital images made under low-light conditions. It may appear hovering near a ceiling, over a bed, or inside a car. Impressive pictures of light anomalies may be viewed at several websites.

Generally, light anomalies should not be readily accepted as evidence of spirit presence unless there is corroborating evidence derived from other technical devices. Corroborating evidence might also be found in psychic impressions experienced at the time and place that the light anomaly was captured. For example, psychic impressions of intense emotions, sobbing, cries for help, or screaming might be obtained while standing in an old hospital room as a photographer captures a picture of an orb hovering over the bed.

**Audio Recording Techniques**

Digital recorders provide an inexpensive way to obtain audio evidence of paranormal activity. The popular term for this is "electronic voice phenomena" or EVP. EVP may include the sound of moving objects, such as doors, windows, or glass objects; whistling; sobbing; laughter; screams; humming; footsteps; explosions; musical notes; or tapping and knocking. Given this wide variety of sounds, I have proposed that the term EVP be replaced by EAP, electronic audio phenomena, and defined as any audio recording that cannot be attributed to normal phenomena.

The ghost hunter may record EAP while remaining stationary at a site, such as within a prison cell or treatment room in an asylum, or while walking around a location. This is called an EAP or EVP sweep. Generally, questions are asked to which spirits may respond. These questions should be simple and follow an invitation for any spirits present to communicate. Typical questions include:

"What is your name?"

"Did you die here?"

"How old are you?"

"Do you want me to leave?"

"Why are you here?"

In most cases, spirit responses cannot be heard by the ghost hunter when they occur but they may be discovered on the audio recording during playback. Typically, responses are brief, rarely lasting more than a few seconds. Vocalizations sometimes have amazing clarity but most often they are unintelligible and, as with other sounds, rarely repeated in subsequent recordings.

Often, EAP consists of nonvocal sounds. Musical instruments, slamming doors, gunshots, footsteps, and tapping sounds may be evoked by the ghost hunter's questions. Ghosts that are unable to generate vocalizations may resort to these sounds as the only means of communication. You may ask, "Why are you here?" On playback, the recording may reveal the sound of footsteps moving away from the microphone. In this instance, the ghost may have been troubled by the question and decided to leave.

Since most EAP can be heard only during playback, ghost hunters should review recordings every 5-10 minutes during the investigation, rather than waiting until the investigation is completed. This will enable the identification of hot spots for spirit activity that may be investigated more thoroughly.

**Video Recording**

Video recorders offer a wide variety of recording features from time-lapse to auto-start/stop and autofocus. These features enable you to make surveillance-type recordings over many hours while you are off-site. Consult your user's manual for low-light recording guidelines and always use a tripod and long-duration battery packs.

**High-Tech Equipment**

You can purchase high-tech devices such as electromagnetic field detectors, infrared thermometers, barometers, and motion detectors at your local electronics store or over the Internet. Good sources for high-tech ghost-hunting equipment are the Society for Paranormal Investigation, The GhostHunter Store, and the EMF Safety Superstore.

Inexpensive, battery-operated motion detectors can be placed at several locations within an investigation site. Some of these allow users to select an audio signal or a silent flashing light signal and connect the output to a central monitor. These devices work by measuring optical or acoustical changes in the environment.

Infrared thermometers have been used to search for cold spots that may signal the presence of a g host. While these devices are widely utilized, and sometimes displayed on paranormal TV shows, they are often used incorrectly. They cannot assess changes in the temperature of clear air because of its very low density and minimal reflection of infrared energy. However, infrared thermometers can detect the surface temperature of solid objects, liquids, dense gases, and clouds.

The most advanced and expensive piece of equipment used by ghost hunters is the FLIR imaging device. FLIR is an acronym for forward-looking infrared. FLIRs detect thermal energy in the infrared range. The FLIR lens focuses the scene on a vast array of sensors that produce thousands of simultaneous measurements of thermal energy. Software then assembles the thermal measurements into a mosaic or picture that is displayed on a handheld video screen.

FLIR systems can see through atmospheric obscurants such as smoke or fog and in total darkness. Ghost hunters use them to detect spirits that do not generate an image within the human visual spectrum. Theoretically, when spirits appear on our plane they draw energy from the environment, creating a cold spot. A FLIR will detect subtle changes in temperature and depict the shape of the cold spot on the video screen. When the shape of the cold spot is humanoid, ghost hunters claim they have evidence that a ghost is present.

Despite the technical sophistication and expense of FLIRs, the images they produce may be misinterpreted. FLIRs may detect sources of heat or cold created by normal processes not noticed by the user.

Electromagnetic field (EMF) detectors are used by paranormal investigators to detect the presence of ghosts in spite of the lack of scientific evidence that EMF and spirit presence are linked. Ghost hunters who use EMF detectors claim that spikes in a local electromagnetic field are created when a ghost transitions onto our plane of existence. These devices, however, often pick up EMF generated by unseen electrical appliances, faulty wiring in an old house, cell phones, walkie-talkies, video recorders, electric cars, and numerous other sources. EMF detectors may be useful if proper controls are established and all possible sources of natural EMF are identified.

Electronic gadgets can be useful and fun, but unless you have a means of creating a record of the instrument's output or storing images or data in a computer, your reports of light anomalies, apparent paranormal motion of objects, changes in the physical characteristics of the environment, or apparitions will not constitute the kind of hard evidence you need to satisfy skeptics.

Keep in mind that even expensive instruments may produce erroneous data or signals if they are incorrectly calibrated, misused, or improperly maintained. Also, data can be easily misinterpreted if the user does not understand the technical or operating limitations of the device. Using expensive high-tech gadgets does not guarantee accurate results, nor do they validate a ghost hunt as a scientific investigation.

**Very Low-Tech Devices**

Investigators have had great success in detecting spirit activity with common household items. Ghosts often become active when they are irritated by changes in their favored environment. If you tilt a picture hanging on the wall, leave an object in the ghost's favorite chair, or leave a book open, a ghost may straighten the picture, remove the object from his chair, or close the book.

Spirits may be attracted to objects they can manipulate easily. Leave four aces at the top of a deck of cards. A ghost may shuffle them throughout the deck. Ghosts are often attracted to water. A glass left full may later be found empty and the contents wetting the floor. A paper and pencil may be used by a ghost to leave bizarre marks or a legible message. Leave two stacks of coins—10 pennies in each stack—on a stable surface and leave the room for an extended period of time. When you return, the coins may be scattered. If both stacks are scattered, a gust of wind or vibration of the building may account for the change. If one stack remains untouched while the other is scattered, that may be the work of a ghost.

## THE PSYCHIC METHOD

The Psychic Method relies upon your intuition, inner vision, or emotional connection with a deceased person, object, place, or point of time in history. You don't have to be a trained psychic to use this approach. All of us have some capacity to tap into unseen dimensions and use some of the psychic tools described in my book *Psychic: Use Your Psychic Powers to Experience Ghosts*. Your ability to use psychic tools for successful ghost hunting depends upon three factors: your innate ability, receptivity, and sensitivity.

You may have an ability to successfully use psychic tools in a ghost hunt if you are one of those people who can readily identify isolated places within a room that elicit a chilling feeling or recognize that there is something bizarre or paranormal about the spot. The ability to identify these places must include a capacity to sort out your impressions, clear your mind of extraneous thoughts and distractions, and focus your attention on the particular point from which a paranormal impression emanates.

You may have sufficient receptivity to effectively use psychic tools if you feel more intensely connected to a place or past era than others or often feel mentally transported to another era. Do you often get that curious feeling that some unseen person is standing behind you, watching you, or touching you? When you touch an artifact, such as a weapon, do you get the impression that you have become aware of information about the object or its user? If so, you are receptive to unseen dimensions and likely to have success hunting ghosts with psychic tools.

You may have exceptional sensitivity if you get vivid impressions of emotions in specific locations within allegedly haunted places. Do you walk into a historic building and get that eerie feeling that something or someone from the past still lingers there? Do you get a sense of "vibes" of fear, anger, pain, or suffering when you visit historic places or places known to be haunted? If so, you may be sensitive to residual energies from past events, emotions that played out in a particular place, or the actions of people who have been gone from the scene for decades. Sensitive people frequently detect a distant time or a voice, sound, touch, or texture of another dimension often described as a change in atmosphere.

Your sensitivity will pay off in a ghost hunt if your investigation is aimed at strong paranormal imprints or attachments of spirits. Strong imprints and attachments are indicated by the frequency, duration, and consistency of the detected paranormal activity that reportedly occurs at a particular place. The strongest imprints are created by intense emotions such as fear, rage, jealousy, revenge, or loss, especially if they were repetitive over long periods prior to death. Biographical research may reveal this kind of information, particularly if personal letters or diaries are examined. Old newspaper articles, suicide notes, and photographs are useful too.

You may enhance your sensitivity by developing and expressing empathy for the ghost's lingering presence at a haunted site. Empathy can be based on your research, which may reveal information about the entity's personal history and probable emotions, motivations, problems, or unfinished business at the time of death. You may also learn that a ghost may be trapped, confused, or has chosen to remain at a site to protect someone or guard something precious.

Your sensitivity to ghostly environmental imprints and spirit manifestations may also be increased by meditation, the relaxing of one's physical body to eliminate distracting thoughts and tensions and achieve emotional focus. Meditation allows you to concentrate your spiritual awareness on a single subject—a place, entity, or historic moment in time. Markers of time or season, artifacts or implements, furniture and doorways are a few suggestions of things to focus on. As the subject comes into focus, you can add information obtained from your research, information that relates specifically to the spirit under investigation such as the type of device used for a suicide or murder, favored book, musical instrument, etc. Through this process, you will become aware of unseen dimensions of the world around you, creating a feeling that you have moved through time to a distant era.

Keep in mind that it is possible to be in a meditative state while appearing quite normal. The process is simple and easy to learn. The variety of meditation methods is broad and beyond the scope of this book. You may locate a meditation methodology online that works well for you but practice it before visiting a haunted location.

**Psychic Tools**

**Clairaudience:** The perception of sounds generated by paranormal sources is called clairaudience. The term is derived from the French, meaning "clear hearing." People with this ability may hear the voices of spirits who are trying to communicate or the sounds of events that occurred years or decades earlier. The latter are most often environmental imprints created by intense repetitive emotions or events that had a strong emotional component.

**Clairsentience:** Some ghosts manifest by creating impressions of physical sensations in receptive people that may include a feeling of being touched. Others are accompanied by fragrances or odors. The ability to perceive or detect these physical sensations and smells that do not truly exist on this plane is called clairsentience. Signature perfumes or the fragrance of favorite flowers can help you identify a ghost. Odors such as cigars, oranges, and hemp are common ghostly manifestations. Sometimes, ghost hunters encounter the noxious odors of rotting meat or burning flesh.

**Clairvoyance:** Information or impressions may be received from objects or spirits without the use of "normal" senses. The process is called clairvoyance and usually refers to visual impressions. People who see ghosts, whether the image is lifelike or merely a human-shaped fragment of a shadow, are clairvoyant. Visual information or impressions may include light anomalies, amorphous clouds, or objects. Since clairvoyance is limited to "real time" events, any visual experience suggests a ghost is present at the moment.

**Retrocognition**: Perception of visual or audio impressions of events from the past is a form of clairvoyance or clairaudience called retrocognition. Psychic Derek Acorah dramatically portrayed his retrocognition ability during ghost investigations in the popular TV show *Most Haunted.* If you watched my TV shows *Ghosts of the Queen Mary* and *Legends of Alcatraz,* you've seen me perform retrocognition.

**Psychometry**: Psychometry is the perception of information embedded in the electromagnetic field of an object. Its owner's use may have altered its EMF and left durable traces of the user's energy, much like a fingerprint, especially if intense emotions were associated with frequent use. Information about an object or one of its users may be obtained by psychically gifted or skilled people using this tool. First described in 1842 by Joseph R. Buchanan, the process has been used in séances, ghost hunts, and crime scene investigations. After a few minutes of handling an object, practitioners of psychometry get visual impressions or become aware of information that cannot be the result of logical inference (piecing things together from clues you might have). Ghost hunters can use psychometry to gain information about a spirit's affinity for a chair or a book or why it moves a particular glass or key. Any object that has reportedly been moved by a ghost should be examined by psychometry. Investigators may get clues about the identity of the ghost or reasons for its haunting activity.

During your visits to old theatres, bars, and tunnels, perform psychometry by grasping the old doorknobs with your hands, lay upon the bed once used by a patient, and handle artifacts at the site such as a water faucet, metal cup, chair, etc.

## SEARCHING FOR GHOSTS

The foremost rule for successful ghost hunting is to be patient! Professional ghost hunters sometimes wait several days, weeks, even months before achieving contact with a ghost. Others have observed full-body apparitions when they least expected it, while concentrating fully on some other activity. Regardless of the depth of your research or preparation, you need to be patient. The serious ghost hunter will anticipate that several trips to a haunted site may be required before some sign of ghostly activity is observed.

Remaining stationary within a cell, treatment room, morgue, or other confirmed location is often productive. If a ghost is known to have a favorite chair, bed, or other place within a room, he may manifest there. If your ghost is not known to appear at a specific place within a room or an outdoors area, position yourself to gain the broadest view of the site. A corner of a room is optimal because it allows the ghost unobstructed motion while avoiding the impression of a trap set by uninvited people who occupy his favorite space.

Once you are on site, meditation may help you focus and maintain empathy for your ghost. Investigate sounds, even common sounds, as the ghost attempts to communicate with you. Pay attention to your own sensations or perceptions, such as the odd feeling that someone is watching you, standing close by, or touching you. A ghost may be hunting you!

CHAPTER 2

# Central Portland

Known as the Rose City since 1905, Portland has had several less flattering nicknames. Before Francis Pettygrove won the coin toss in 1845 that gave him the right to name the tiny settlement on the Willamette River "Portland," this place was known as "Stumptown" due to the many tree stumps that remained after timber had been harvested to build the first homes and piers. Unimpressed visitors also called it "the Clearing" and "Mudtown." Later in the 19th century, the infamous underground industry of kidnapping gave rise to the moniker "Shanghai City." Early in the 20th century that nefarious business was eradicated and the city became known for its culture, economic power, educational institutions, and architecture. Nine bridges spanning the Willamette River have inspired the unavoidable nickname "Bridge City," while other features encouraged "Rip City," "Little Beirut," "Cloud City," "Forbidden City," and "Portlandia." Some ghost hunters have offered "Spook City" in recognition of the many haunted places that attract visitors from all over the U.S.

While many of Portland's most famous ghosts transitioned into the spirit world in the 19th century, there are plenty of modern ghosts to be found in fancy hotels, unique bars and restaurants, and sites where tragic accidents and criminal activity occurred. The well-known Shanghai Tunnels are a good place to start your Portland adventure because docents will begin with an overview of the city's dark history, which includes many downtown buildings. After visiting haunted locations in central Portland, take a short drive to the Pittock Mansion for a spectacular vista of the Rose City. Then drive north through the thriving Northwest District, also known as "Snob Hill" and "Trendy Third," to the site of the horrific Vanport Flood and Portland's northwest industrial area, marked by the St. Johns Bridge, where the ghost of a young murder victim keeps local legends alive and ghost hunters busy. If you plan to spend a night or two in downtown Portland, consider one of the city's haunted hotels if you truly want to have a cozy experience with some fascinating ghosts.

## GHOSTS OF SHANGHAI VICTIMS

Shanghai Tunnels Tours
Meet at: 120 NW Third Avenue
Portland 97209
503-622-4798
www.portlandtunnels.com

Many of the cities I've investigated sit upon an underground maze of tunnels that once housed gambling and opium dens, rooms for storing contraband such as sex slaves and liquor, cells for keeping kidnapped persons, and lockers for weapons and explosives. Early residents of Seattle, San Francisco, Sacramento, Boston, Savannah, Chicago, and Baltimore built these underground cities to keep their nefarious businesses away from the eyes of local citizens, who usually had no idea what horrific enterprises were conducted a few feet below a fancy hotel or restaurant where they enjoyed the finest accommodations and cuisine these booming cities could offer. With the collusion of police and other city officials, who were often paid to ignore kidnappings, prostitution, rape, murder, gambling, and trafficking in drugs and humans, these businesses thrived for many years before cave-ins, intrusion of city projects such as new sewers, fires, floods, and disease put an end to them. Today, these underground cities attract curious tourists and ghost hunters, but most of them have been sealed or nearly destroyed, leaving only fragments of passageways and dusty rooms where many people died of disease or assault, miles from home, in the company of ruthless people who gave them no thought as their lives ended. The infamous Shanghai Tunnels system of Portland is probably the country's best surviving example of the astounding network of rooms and tunnels that made the underground illegal activity possible. These tunnels may also be the most haunted place in the Pacific Northwest.

The Shanghai Tunnels that run beneath the streets of modern Portland started in 1850 as modest passageways between basements, usually connecting businesses owned by the same person. The subterranean link was developed to enable the movement and storage of goods and passage of workers without having to cross busy, muddy streets. Within a few years, several tunnels became connected, creating an expansive maze of tunnels lined with brick and shored up with heavy beams. It is believed that the tunnel system became so extensive that it linked many waterfront warehouses and docks with buildings as far west as NW 19th near NW Davis Street. Historical research has revealed major tunnels that stretched from the current intersection of West Burnside Street and NW 19th Street to Bunco Docks, Wooden Nickel Docks, Turk's Hotel for Sailors, Bosh Wharf, and Greenhorn Dock. These tunnels also joined a subterranean thoroughfare that ran parallel to the shore of the Willamette River, connecting warehouses, flophouses, and bars. The seclusion of these tunnels and the rooms they linked, and the ease by which entry was regulated, fostered their rapid transition from convenient passageways to networks of crime and depravity. By 1855, the underground had become a veritable city, with kitchens, storage rooms, bunkrooms, gambling dens, rooms for numerous stables of prostitutes, and cells in which kidnapped persons were kept.

Portland's Shanghai Tunnels get their name from the business of abducting drunk or drugged men and selling them to the captains of waiting ships who were desperate for crewmen. Men called "crimps" would circulate through the bars and hotels searching for potential victims. Initially, the crimps would befriend the lonely sailor and offer to buy drinks. With the collusion of the bartender, the drink was laced with a barbiturate that quickly rendered the victim nearly unconscious. The unfortunate man was then positioned over a trapdoor, called a "dead fall," and dropped into a basement, where others employed in the business would take the man's shoes and toss him in a cell until he could be transported though the tunnels to a waiting ship. It is said that many men died in the damp, dark cells of exposure, starvation, drug overdose, or injuries before they could be moved to the docks.

At the docks, a quick deal with unscrupulous captains usually netted $50 per man. Hours or days after the ship had sailed, the men would awake from their drugged or drunken stupor only to find themselves pressed into service as sailors. Apparently, the practice was rampant in the Far East and was given the moniker "shanghai" for the city in which it started. It is said that Portland's shanghai business continued until 1941, when World War II created tens of thousands of legal jobs on merchant ships and naval vessels. Some historians believe that as many as 1,500 men were shanghaied each year from 1855 to 1941.

The tunnels were also used to house women kidnapped from the streets. Crimps posing as missionaries or police would spot women newly arrived in town and recommend a particular boardinghouse or hotel. Once checked in, the women would be drugged and transported to underground cells, where they underwent days or weeks of deprivation and psychological attacks. In many cases, they were told that they must work in the sex industry or their family would be informed that they had taken up a depraved life in Portland. Seeking to avoid an unbearable reputation, they became easily managed and locked into a sordid life that often ended with a very early death.

Historians surmise that none of these horrific enterprises could have continued without the collusion of the police department and other public officials. Word did circulate around the city, however, that waterfront bars and hotels were

*Remnants of bunk beds, jail cells, and kitchens stand as dusty, dark reminders of the misery of life in Portland's Shanghai Tunnels.*

dangerous places even for able-bodied seamen, lumberjacks, and ranchers who had landed in town with a lot of money, eager for a good time. Some stories surfaced that were horrifying, but others were somewhat humorous. One crimp was so eager to make a few bucks that he wrapped a blanket around a wooden statue of a Native American—known as a "cigar-store Indian"—and sold the "sailor" to the captain of a ship about to set sail. Hours later, when the deceit was discovered, it so angered the captain that he threw the statue overboard. It is said that a dredge brought it to the surface 60 years later. Crimps often transported "unconscious" captives aboard a ship knowing that the unresponsive person was actually dead. It has been said that many captains were far at sea before they learned that half their crew were deceased.

Nearly 90 years of misery, fear, anger, hopelessness, hatred, and unspeakable cruelty left some indelible imprints in the tunnels that are easy to detect. Some of these are intense, leaving unsuspecting tourists dazed and frightened by the emotions that suddenly sweep through them while they snap a few pictures or chat with friends. The dusty, still air is often filled with soft moaning, sobbing, screams, gasps for air, and pleas for help. Disembodied footsteps, the squeaking hinges of cell doors, heavy breathing, grunting, and the crack of a whip are common audio experiences.

*This ghost hunter seeks EVP from the ghosts of sailors who were drugged and jailed here until they could be smuggled aboard a ship.*

Ghosts fill these spaces, rising up from dusty cells, stacks of wooden bunk beds, the floor beneath the dead fall, or the dark passages not open to tourists. The most frequently sighted ghosts in these tunnels are those of crimps who may be condemned to remain in the dark, damp spaces where they ruined the lives of thousands of men and women. Psychics and others with sufficient sensitivity and receptivity describe the crimps as large shadowy figures, very dark, with red eyes. When they appear, even the least sensitive person gets a very uneasy feeling, as the atmosphere becomes dense and cold. Often, while listening intently to docents, tourists sense a large presence behind them as a crimp hovers over their shoulder.

A large group of ghosts, thought to be the crew of the ill-fated ship *Jennifer Jo,* shows up occasionally in various parts of the tunnels. They skulk about, searching for the crimps who pressed them into service. Legend says that a large number of men, all beaten, starved, and drugged, were hauled unconscious aboard the *Jennifer Jo,* a ship desperate for a crew. Not willing to wait for the shanghaied men to awaken, the captain set sail from Bunco's Dock in the middle of the night, only to sink somewhere in the Columbia River. All hands went down with the ship, including the shanghaied crew who were still locked belowdecks. Angry and seething with pain, these men manifest in the tunnels by laying a wet hand on the shoulder of tourists.

Not all the ghosts in these tunnels are angry or in pain. The ghost of a young boy, said to be about nine years old, has been spotted by many witnesses as he moves from a bunk-bed cell to a hallway and then vanishes. Some ghost hunters report that he carries a bucket or chamber pot. It is likely that this boy was an orphan who found a job in the tunnels emptying the large volume of waste produced by all the men and women held captive there.

With rare exceptions, access to the Shanghai Tunnels is possible only by joining a scheduled tour. Knowledgeable docents provide plenty of anecdotes and history, and a few ghost stories, while allowing tourists time to snap pictures and perform EVP sweeps. Despite the large number of people in a tour, ghostly manifestations are common. Spirits come forward and speak up as if they wish to get the attention of anyone who might free them of their miserable existence. Be patient and be ready.

## GHOST OF THE MURDERED PROSTITUTE

Old Town Pizza
226 NW Davis Street
Portland 97209
503-222-9999
www.oldtownpizza.com

For more than 100 years, the ghost of Nina (pronounced *Nigh-na*) has wandered through the old Merchant Hotel building, but no one has determined why she remains near the site of her murder. At times, her presence is indicated only by the faint fragrance of her signature perfume, the swishing sound of her long skirt, or a sweet voice whispering a word or two. When she has sufficient energy, and potential witnesses have the necessary level of sensitivity, Nina appears in a black dress with her long dark hair pulled back in a tight bun. She apparently likes what she sees in the renovated building, because she walks through Old Town Pizza without an expression of distress and sometimes smiles at astonished patrons. Ghost hunters have captured several light anomalies in digital images and a few fascinating EVP that may be Nina's manifestations. Staff members of the restaurant report that they have left out a bowl containing Scrabble tiles overnight only to find that a ghostly hand has arranged particular letters in curious but intelligible messages.

Nina is often sought in a small booth that was once the elevator shaft of the Merchant Hotel. Her name, allegedly inscribed by her ghostly hand, can be seen on one of the bricks in a wall of the booth, although there is no unequivocal historical record that a woman by that name ever lived or worked in the building. Local psychics, however, report frequent interactions with this ghost that affirm her name is, indeed, Nina and her life was tragically cut short by murder.

In 1881, the Merchant Hotel was conceived as a state-of-the-art hotel that was so advanced in its architecture, plumbing, gas lighting, and other conveniences that construction spanned four years. Built by lumber barons Adolph, Louis, and

Theodore Nicolai, the place opened in 1885 and immediately attracted clientele from the city's high society who sought the best drinks and food and most luxurious rooms for private liaisons. It is unlikely that Nina lived or worked in the fine rooms and suites of the Merchant Hotel, however. Her life was that of a prostitute, possibly kidnapped as a teenager and kept in the dark rooms of the hotel's basement that connected with Portland's infamous underground city.

Legend says that Nina was contacted by local missionaries who promised her a safe escape from pimps and guards if she would reveal the identities of the men who operated the wretched prostitution, gambling, and shanghai business in the underground caverns that stretched from the basement of the Merchant Hotel to numerous other buildings and, ultimately, the waterfront. Feeling assured that she would be

*It is said that the ghost of Nina, murdered at this spot, scratched her name on this brick.*

safely delivered from her miserable life, Nina agreed to give up the information. This risky plan was discovered, however, by someone associated with her captors, so she was summoned to the third floor of the hotel under the pretext that she was to entertain a special guest. Upon arriving at the meeting, Nina was accosted and thrown down the elevator shaft to her death

I could find no historical record of the murder, but local ghost hunters and purveyors of urban legends insist it is true. The killer, of course, was never captured or identified. Many years later, the hydraulic elevator was removed, leaving the shaft where Nina died as an air vent. Today, a popular booth in Old Town Pizza occupies the spot, and patrons often linger there for hours hoping to have an encounter with Nina.

I found her there on one occasion. After I sat alone for nearly an hour, the space around me was suddenly filled with the fragrance of a perfume and the sound of a swishing skirt. Instantly, the small space felt crowded, as a faint voice said in a lilting, melodic tone, "I'm here." During other visits to Old Town Pizza, my companion and I have heard the tapping sound of a woman's boot on the floor at a time when no one close by was moving about. Again, the fragrance of a pungent perfume filled the space around us before suddenly vanishing.

## SUICIDE GHOST

The Heathman Hotel
1001 SW Broadway
Portland 971001
503-241-4100 or (877) 239-0882
www.heathmanhotel.com

The number three seems to be linked to a haunting at the Heathman Hotel. For many years, rooms that end with the number have been the site of intense paranormal activity that experts have attributed to a suicide that took place in room 1003. In 1999, a celebrity psychic known to me visited the Heathman and perceived the presence of a woman about

30 years old who jumped to her death from a window. Some speculate that the woman cursed the hotel as she fell to the ground, passing rooms with numbers that ended with a three. Her reason for cursing the hotel and haunting these rooms is unknown. My research failed to uncover an official record of a person committing suicide at this address. The place opened in 1927, however, and old records are difficult to locate. Also, powerful businessmen often had great success burying a story that might harm the reputation of a successful enterprise.

In room 803, an apparition manifests that is most often vague and transparent. On some occasions, the manifestation reveals more details and resembles a woman with shoulder-length, brown, curly hair and a sharp chin. Details sometimes include a facial expression of deep anguish or fear. The paranormal activity in this room has been described as poltergeist manifestations, but it seems clear that this is incorrect terminology. Experts attribute poltergeist activity to a living person who is emotionally or mentally disturbed. When that person, termed the "agent," is removed from the scene, all paranormal activity ceases. In the case of room 803, there is no single, identifiable, living person consistently at the scene when bizarre events occur. These events include intense cold spots, sounds that include sobbing and moaning, and the movement of personal objects to strange locations. In addition, guests have reported returning to the room after an absence of a few hours only to find that furniture has been moved, towels used, and glasses of water placed at various locations. Similar but less intense activity has been reported in room 703.

In every one of the "3" rooms, guests have called the front desk to report an eerie presence. Sometimes a face stares at them from out of the darkness. When the log for the electronic lock is checked, there is no indication of inappropriate entry.

The Heathman Hotel should not be confused with its predecessor of the same name. The original Heathman was completed in 1926 at the corner of SW Park and SW Salmon. Designed to cater to wealthy timber barons and politicians, it was so successful that construction of the New Heathman Hotel was begun early in 1927. Standing 10 stories tall and faced with brick, it was even more luxurious than its namesake. It opened on December 17, 1927, with the expectation that it would attract the growing population of wheeler-dealers in Portland. The party staged to celebrate the hotel's opening was a grand event. All 1,200 workmen who built the place were invited, in addition to the members of wealthy society who were expected to make the business a success. By some accounts, this party was a wild affair with guests visiting many of the rooms and, perhaps, conducting several private parties behind closed doors. Liquor flowed generously despite Prohibition, which may have caused the happy event to lead to an accident, suicide, or something sinister. It isn't too much of a stretch to wonder if a private party turned into something quite negative and, in a drunken stupor, a man tossed an uncooperative woman out a window.

## GHOSTS OF FANCY GUESTS

Benson Hotel
309 SW Broadway
Portland 97205
503-228-2000
www.coasthotels.com/the-benson-hotel

The Benson Hotel is one of a handful of historical hotels that include the Heathman (built 1927), Commodore (built 1925), Imperial (built 1894), and Governor (built 1909). Constructed in 1912 by Simon Benson (1852-1942), and opened on March 5, 1913, the hotel fulfilled his wish to create a world-class hotel in Portland. A philanthropist but always a wise businessman, Benson saw the opportunity to cash in on Portland's population boom, which occurred between the 1905 Lewis and Clark Centennial Exposition and the Great Depression. Today, the 287-room hotel is distinguished by its French Second Empire style, spectacular décor, elegant staircase that conveys guests into a large lobby complete with a huge fireplace, and ornate ceilings from which French chandeliers hang.

Simon Benson occupies a prominent place in Portland history for many reasons. His philanthropy included a gift of $100,000 to the Portland School District to help fund the construction of a polytechnic school. During World War I, the school was used to train soldiers, but in 1919 it officially opened as Benson Polytechnic High School. In 1921, he deeded nine acres of land overlooking the Willamette River that ultimately became Madrona Park. These and many other generous acts were the result of Benson's philosophy: "No one has the right to die and not leave something to the public and for the public good."

Simon Benson may be remembered most for a gift of $10,000 to the city of Portland used to install 20 bronze public drinking fountains. Being opposed to the consumption of alcohol, even after Prohibition, he was often incensed by drunks who wandered the streets. Since many of these men claimed they drank beer or liquor because they were thirsty, Benson believed that the installation of water fountains might quench their thirst and reduce their visits to Portland's many bars. Many of those fountains, dubbed Benson's Bubblers, are still in use today.

The ghostly image of a well-dressed gentleman has been seen descending the Benson Hotel's staircase to the lobby before moving into the lounge, where guests often enjoy a drink or two. He is said to cast a disapproving look at people before disappearing. Moments later, guests discover that their drinks have been toppled. This kind of behavior recalls Benson's aversion to alcohol. Ghost hunters might trigger the manifestation of this ghost by taking a seat in the lounge and ordering a tall drink.

A stylishly dressed female ghost wanders the hallway on several floors. Witnesses have reported that she wears a turquoise dress and walks with a graceful gait. She often appears lifelike, but when astonished guests turn to watch her, she vanishes. This ghost is most often sighted on the seventh and 12fth floors and in the lobby.

Several guests at the Benson have posted reports of their experiences with the ghost of a little boy. Appearing to be three years old, he shows up at the bedside, looking at guests who are about to drift off to sleep. One woman reported that she touched the child and he felt warm and solid. Apparently, he likes to play, because he makes faces described as "scary" and pulls blankets from the bed.

In researching hotels and inns for paranormal activity, most ghost hunters look for a history of untimely natural death, suicide, or murder. At the Benson, there is only one official demise, that of Mitch Mitchell (1947-2008). He was the drummer for rhythm-and-blues and rock performer Jimi Hendrix (1942-70). Many years after Hendrix's death, Mitchell was featured in the 2008 Experience Hendrix Tour. After four weeks on the road with performances in 18 cities, he was showing signs of slowing down and exhibited an unsteady gait attributed to many years of alcohol-related illness. On the night of November 12, Mitchell retired to his room at the Benson, only to be found dead at three o'clock in the morning by a hotel employee. The Multnomah County medical examiner ruled that the death was due to natural causes.

*Ghosts dressed in early-20th-century clothing have been spotted descending this elegant staircase to the lobby of the Benson Hotel.*

Some writers believe that Mitchell haunts the Benson Hotel, manifesting as a child because he was a child actor in England and that was the happiest period of his life. I don't believe that this assertion is valid, however. Mitchell achieved stardom as a teenager on a TV show in the UK called *Jennings and Derbyshire* and landed a leading role in the 1960 British film *Bottoms Up*. If he haunts the hotel as an earlier version of himself, it would likely be as a teenager, not as a three-year-old child.

## GHOSTS OF THE OLD HOTEL

Meier and Frank Building
The Nines Hotel
525 SW Morrison Street
Portland 97204
503-222-9996
www.thenines.com

The ghosts that haunt this luxury hotel are linked to the former Meier and Frank department store. Constructed in 1913 with major additions in 1915 and 1932, the building seems to have ghosts on several floors connected to the early history of the store. Meier and Frank, founded in Portland in 1857, was the flagship store and headquarters of what was to become the largest retailer west of the Mississippi. Acquired by May Department Stores in 1966, the enterprise ultimately ended up in the hands of Macy's. Since 2008, the Nines Hotel has occupied the top nine floors, while the lower floors are retail space for Macy's.

The 17-story, glazed terra-cotta building, located in downtown Portland, replaced an earlier structure built in 1898. Conceived by Sigmund Frank (1850-1910), the current building featured an astounding 11 acres of retail space. Since Sigmund died before its completion, there is speculation that he roams the floors to this day, admiring the huge building he envisioned. Aaron Meier (1831-89) may wander about the place too. At the age of 26, he founded the retail business in a 35-by-50-foot mercantile store at 137 Front Street at a time when Portland had a population of only 1,300. In 1878, the Great Portland Fire destroyed the store together with 20 downtown blocks. A partnership with Emil Frank, Sigmund's brother, enabled him to rebuild at the same site. In 1888, Emil left the business, and Sigmund headed the organization after Meier died in 1889.

Long after Sigmund's death, Meier and Frank executives hired a 21-year-old man named Clark Gable (1901-60) to work as a necktie salesman. Clark stayed on the job only a few years while he gained experience in local theater.

Among the credible accounts of ghostly activity in the building is that of former Meier and Frank executive Kay Hale. Working late one night, Kay decided to sleep on a sofa in her office rather than drive to her home. Much of the floor where her office was located was filled with old merchandise awaiting shipment to other stores or to the manufacturer. Sometime during the night, she was awakened by loud noises, as if a crew of men were moving heavy boxes around. Occasionally, the sound of the freight elevator gate moving up and down echoed across the floor and through the thin walls of Kay's office. Several times, she heard the elevator move as if it were descending to lower floors. During all of this commotion, Kay heard several voices speaking sharply in hushed tones and sometimes laughing. Too frightened to open her door to see if a night crew had arrived to move merchandise, Kay locked her door and waited until the noise had abated. In the morning, she inquired if a crew had, indeed, worked through the night on her floor. She became nervous as fellow executives denied any knowledge of a work order that might account for Kay's experience. To make this episode even more chilling, Kay found that none of the boxes on her floor had been moved, yet she had heard men working for hours. No one in the building could offer information that might explain the ghostly sounds that Kay had heard. When she approached a security guard for his opinion, he said, "It must have been the ghosts."

The Macy's shoe department on the second floor has been the site of some interesting paranormal activity. For a period of several weeks, when store staff members arrived in the morning, they found that several pairs of shoes had been mixed in the most bizarre way. It was assumed this was a practical joke until surveillance video revealed shoes flying off a shelf and socks tossed into the air.

The most disturbing account comes from members of a cleaning crew who worked in the kitchen of the eighth-floor Georgian Room Restaurant one night. They all witnessed bizarre paranormal activity that included utensils flying across the room, objects sliding off the counters, drawers opening and slamming shut, and supplies such as flour and salt blasting into the air. Some of the workers reported that they perceived an evil presence that wanted them to leave the floor. When asked to describe this entity, one man said it was "too terrible to describe." This experience was so frightening that the entire cleaning crew quit the job.

The Georgian Room is beautifully furnished and the food is great. In April of 2014, I spoke to a person who had worked there for three years. She denied having a paranormal experience in the kitchen or any other place within the restaurant. She did, however, tell me about the experiences of her co-workers. Apparently, they never encountered anything malevolent, but there does seem to be a spirit in the kitchen that likes things put back in their proper place.

The library is a spectacular room decorated in an Old World style with leather furniture and built-in walnut bookcases. I experienced a benevolent presence there. This spirit was that of an elderly man who seemed quite pleased with the energy of the place. I suspect this ghost is Sigmund Frank.

## GHOSTS OF THE MURDERED MOB

Scooter McQuade's Restaurant and Bar
1321 SW Washington Street
Portland 97205
503-248-1060

In the latter part of the 19th century, the building that houses Scooter McQuade's Restaurant and Bar was an integral part of the shanghai industry. Drunk or drugged men were dropped through a dead fall to the basement below and kept until they could be transported through the tunnels to the waterfront. Throughout Prohibition (1920-33), the shanghai business was much less active, but the dark spaces underneath downtown bars and the tunnels that connected them were filled with bootleggers who stored contraband whiskey and beer. With so much booze, parties in the tunnels were quite frequent, despite the dark and dingy atmosphere. Urban legend tells us that one night in the 1920s, a large group of revelers was attacked by a rival gang wearing stolen police uniforms. As the assailants fired tommy guns and swung axes, the panicked crowd ran through a progressively narrowing tunnel until they created a human plug that would deny anyone safe egress. It is said that the attackers killed everyone and then smashed barrels of whiskey, leaving a telltale odor in the basement for decades.

A century later, paranormal investigators and unsuspecting patrons of this popular bar often encounter a frightened mob of spirits as they emerge from the cellar and dash to the door before vanishing. Witnesses describe these ghosts as angry or scared, glowing humanoid shapes. Some of them are quite lifelike and glare at astonished patrons as they knock over drinks and cause chairs to scoot across the floor. Psychics who try to communicate with these ghosts report that many of these spirits are in a "snarky mood."

A group of ghost hunters staged a formal investigation of the basement and experienced some amazing audio phenomena. Pressing their ears to the bricks that now seal the tunnel, these investigators reported hearing moans, terrified cries, and loud taps that may have been gunshots. The sounds were so clear that ghost hunters had the very strong impression that they started some distance down the tunnel and then grew louder as the ghostly mob approached the brick wall.

## GHOSTS OF THE JITTERBUG DANCERS

Crystal Ballroom
1332 West Burnside Street

Portland 97209
503-225-0047
www.crystalballroompdx.com

Ghostly dancers may still gyrate across the floor of the Crystal Ballroom, oblivious to the passage of time and numerous changes in the style of music and entertainment offered at this iconic venue. Built in 1914 and opened as the Cotillion Hall, the place has staged grand balls, dance recitals, beat poetry readings, and concerts with music ranging from folk to blues to rock. In the 1920s, Portland's citizens paid a nickel to spend the evening square dancing on the third floor. The only refreshment available was apple cider, due to Prohibition. That didn't stop dancers from creating so much revelry that the ballroom became an official venue of the "Roaring Twenties," complete with police raids.

Early in the 1930s, owner Dad Watson died, leaving the place in the hands of Ralph Farrier, who renamed it the Crystal Ballroom. Farrier continued weekly square dances until the mid-1950s, but he is credited with expanding the ballroom offerings to a wide variety of entertainment. In the 1960s, famous acts such as Marvin Gaye, Ike and Tina Turner, and James Brown performed. Later, Gregg Allman, Billy Idol, and the Grateful Dead appeared there, but from the 1970s to the mid-1990s, the place was essentially closed. Eventually, space was rented to artists and private parties were staged, but squatters and vandals almost ruined the venue. Fortunately, in 1997 the McMenamin brothers bought the building and made extensive renovations that included a bar and restaurant on the first floor, a dance floor on the second floor, and a huge ballroom on the third floor. The décor is beautiful with flamboyant wall sconces and light fixtures, peculiar paintings, and huge windows that offer a view of West Burnside Street. People who come there for music and dance seem to easily pick up on the energy created by a century of music and joy. Social scientists call this phenomenon "the power of place."

People who work in this building have spotted apparitions of men and women in clothing typical of the 1920s and '30s. Some of these ghostly images move about in a style of dance called the Jitterbug. The term is early-20th-century slang for the tremors sometimes seen in alcoholics (delirium tremens). Bodily motions are somewhat chaotic and often don't conform to the rhythm of accompanying music. The term "Jitterbug" is often applied to swing dancers or those dancing the "Jive." One dancer described it as "cutting loose and going crazy." The Jitterbug is a high-energy dance that is fun and thrilling, sometimes giving people the greatest joy of their young lives. So it's no wonder that ghosts have returned to the Crystal Ballroom to relive those precious times.

Staff members also hear crowds of people talking and laughing, both men and women. Unexplained sounds often include footsteps and the sliding of shoe leather across the dance floor. Sensitives, including myself, perceive intense energy emanating from the brick walls of the building. It is likely that the minerals of the bricks have "recorded" sounds and images of musicians and dancers that play back at times. The energy of the ballroom may enable ghosts to manifest as well.

## GHOST OF THE DIMINUTIVE WOMAN

Commodore Grocery
621 SW 16th Avenue
Portland 97205
503-224-9661

Commodore Grocery is a tiny convenience store tucked into one of the basement floors of the stately Commodore Building. Built in 1925, the art deco features of the structure have elements that are strinkingly gothic, making the place seem a little spooky. Several gold-painted bird effigies, mounted on a ledge above the first floor, appear to be cormorants decorated with Inca headgear and contribute to the impression that there is something weird about the place. The main entrance to the building faces SW Morrison, but the grocery is entered from SW 16th Avenue. The place is easy to miss, but ghost hunters will find this little store quite interesting because it is haunted by the ghost of a young woman.

People who have worked in the store and regular customers agree that the ghost of Commodore Grocery is a small woman or girl, standing less than five feet tall. She always appears disheveled, wearing a dirty white jacket or hoodie, with her dark hair gathered in a ponytail. Those who have seen her clearest manifestations report that her face looks wrinkled. At times she has given witnesses the impression that she is Native American or Inuit. This ghost usually appears in the rear of the store and remains motionless for several seconds before vanishing. On some occasions, she has been seen dashing back and forth across the central aisle. This ghost never speaks or makes hand gestures to astonished witnesses. She does, however, project intense emotions that sensitive people detect. These emotions

*This quaint neighborhood grocery may be a meeting place for ghosts dating from the days when the Commodore Building was a flophouse for sailors.*

include fear and anxiety, which, in turn, evoke sadness in witnesses, leaving them quite unsettled. Some customers who have watched as this ghost vanished have been frightened by the experience, but there was no impression of malevolence.

There is no record of a robbery involving a shooting or other horrific event in Commodore Grocery that might explain the presence of this ghost. She may have been a homeless person who died nearby and found comfort amid the grocery's humming cooler cases and dim lighting.

Despite its current elegant façade, the Commodore Building was once a flophouse for sailors and other transients. During the 1940s, stories circulated about a ghostly "woman in white" that wandered the halls, creating a trail of cold air while emitting a bizarre laugh. A pharmacy once existed in the space occupied by the grocery, prompting some writers to speculate that this ghost may have had something to do with that business.

## GHOST OF THE MATRON

Pittock Mansion
3229 NW Pittock Drive
Portland 97210
503-823-3623
www.pittockmansion.org

At first, Georgiana Pittock didn't like the idea of moving from downtown Portland to a house perched on the crest of West Hills. She was certain she would feel isolated in this spot that was a half-mile beyond the city limits and accessed only by a very steep, winding road. But the 23-room, Tenino Sandstone mansion surrounded by 46 acres of manicured gardens overlooking Portland convinced her that, at the age of 68, she could make the move and be quite happy in the grand house.

Within days of her arrival, Georgiana set the gardeners to work planting her favorite roses and added personal touches to the interior décor. Her husband, Oregon publisher and industrialist

Henry Pittock, had spared no expense creating the spectacular mansion. He even called in a few political favors to ensure that the place was completed before the end of 1914. A spectacular marble staircase, great windows with panoramic views, chandeliers, a music room, and several bathrooms comprised a home that would be a dream house for anyone on the planet. Modern conveniences included an elevator traveling between the three floors, indirect lighting, intercoms, a walk-in refrigerator, central heating, a dumbwaiter, and a central vacuuming unit.

With a family of children and grandchildren, and frequent social events attended by the finest people in the city, the home was always filled with happiness. Georgiana loved the grand mansion, but her time there was short. In 1918, only four years after settling into the place, she died at the age of 72. Many believe she is still there, unwilling to give up the house on a hill, the things that gave her comfort in her final years, and her beloved gardens.

Henry Pittock (1835-1919) died a year after Georgiana, leaving a legacy of accomplishment that, to many, epitomizes the pioneer spirit. Arriving in Portland in 1853, penniless and only 18 years old, Henry struggled to find work in the printing trade. Over a period of six years, he worked his way up to manager and editor of the weekly *Oregonian* newspaper. By 1861, he owned the newspaper, and over the next four years he made a fortune by publishing news of Civil War battles and Lincoln's assassination ahead of his competitors. After a long career that included political scandal and feuds, he died in his grand mansion on January 28, 1919, at the age of 83, leaving an estate worth nearly $8 million.

Henry may haunt the manse, but many paranormal experts believe that Georgiana is the estate's most active ghost. In 1958, the last Pittock family member moved out and the house stood vacant until 1964, when the city of Portland purchased it to save it from further deterioration. After 15 months of restoration, the Pittock Mansion opened to the public in 1965. About 100,000 people visited the site in 2016.

Since 1965, staff members and visitors have recorded numerous strange events that many attribute to the ghost of

Georgiana. A boyhood picture of Henry Pittock was placed on a mantel in one of the bedrooms, but unseen hands move it from time to time, setting it in locations that were Georgiana's spots. The fragrance of roses often fills a room when fresh flowers are nowhere to be found in the house. Voices of two elderly people, a man and a woman, have often been heard. Typically these are brief bursts of sound in which each voice speaks only two or three words. Slow-moving footsteps have been heard passing over the threshold of several rooms. A few feet beyond the threshold, the sound is no longer heard.

A few fortunate visitors have spotted Georgiana's apparition in the basement, music room, and her bedroom. Occasionally, her image is seen reflected in a mirror, glass covering the paintings, and the windows. Georgiana has been known to create that

*This magnificent mansion stands as a monument to Henry Pittock, who arrived in Portland penniless but became one of the city's wealthiest residents.*

creepy feeling that some unseen being is standing close behind.

Henry manifests infrequently, but his presence is unmistakable. Standing behind people who criticize the opulence of the house or its period furnishings, he creates a strong impression of a man bearing down on the person who dared disparage his great accomplishment. Henry is pleased, however, when people marvel at the beauty of the mansion. He walks about with them as if he is hosting a special tour.

A variety of other paranormal phenomena occurs in the house and gardens. Staff members have turned off the lights for the night only to witness all of them turn on without explanation. Heavy footsteps have been noted leaving the house through a door on the lower floor. These footsteps have been detected in the garden, heading toward a side door of the mansion. On the second floor of the house, window latches have been known to lock and unlock when the weather changes abruptly.

Listen for slow, shuffling footsteps that might be made by an elderly person, and sniff the air for the fragrance of roses. If you detect these phenomena, Georgiana and Henry may be near.

## GHOSTS OF THE SPIES

Wilcox Mansion
931 SW King Avenue
Portland 97205

This spectacular 13,000-square-foot mansion was built in 1893 as a home for industrialist Theodore Burney Wilcox (1856-1918) and his family. Many believe that Theodore's ghost, or that of his son, Theodore, Jr., haunts this place, but my experiences there, and the reports of others, suggest that the paranormal activity may be attributed to the manse's somewhat dark history.

The mansion consists of a basement, two floors constructed of sandstone, and two upper floors of cedar. The interior mahogany woodwork is considered some of the finest in the Pacific Northwest. In fact, a lady I spoke to at the house told me that it is superior to that found in the Pittock Mansion. The place has nine fireplaces, hand-carved decorative trim, and a spectacular staircase. When I last visited, it had undergone renovation into offices and meeting rooms. The radio station KWJJ, which operated in the house since the 1950s, moved a few years earlier, and access is now restricted to those having legitimate business there. That hasn't stopped the circulation of stories about this mansion, however.

Almost 20 years after the death of Theodore, Sr., the manse was leased by a Soviet agency whose staff traveled the Pacific Northwest purchasing farming equipment to ship to the Soviet Union. By 1939, the agents operating out of the house focused on military supplies. Following Germany's invasion of the Soviet Union in 1941, the staff that occupied the Wilcox Mansion was augmented by Soviet spies whose job it was to capture German spies operating on America's West Coast. It has been suggested that many Germans were brought to the house from Portland's docks, as well as San Francisco and Seattle, and then incarcerated in the basement while they were interrogated. This imprisonment may have included the torture and even death of German spies.

Former staff members of the radio station, who worked in cubicles in the basement, reported that it had the disturbing atmosphere of a dungeon, often causing them to seek respite upstairs. Frequently, the apparition of a short, stocky figure would be seen floating across the room. Invariably, this figure would move to the entrance of a tunnel that led to the carriage house. Nothing sinister was ever experienced in the basement, but a woman hired to clean the offices was truly frightened during her shift one night. Moving about the darkened space looking for cleaning supplies, she heard loud, heavy breathing. She raced upstairs and immediately quit.

Employees reported that when the atmosphere in the basement became thick and oppressive, people on the main floor would notice that a huge chandelier would start swinging.

A piano located on the main floor would sound as if an invisible ghost were playing it. Two DJs had numerous sightings of a man walking around the piano. Dressed in a white suit and hat, this fellow gazed upon the piano as if it were a cherished object. This ghost was never menacing, but the DJs reported they were so spooked by his appearance that they locked themselves in their sound booth while working late at night.

The ghost of a female servant has been spotted walking the hallways on the second floor. She wears a black uniform and a white hat and gives witnesses the impression that she is from the 1920s. The apparition of an older man, perhaps 70, has also been spotted moving about the place. This has led to speculation that Theodore Wilcox, Sr., haunts his beloved mansion.

*The Wilcox Mansion has a fascinating history that includes use by Soviet agents during World War II.*

## CHAPTER 3

# East Portland Communities

In the latter part of the 19th century, the Willamette River separated Portland's business center and more affluent neighborhoods from the industrial east shore. The social dichotomy resulted in the eastern half of the city becoming a micro-region where lawlessness was common, social justice was a rare commodity, and misery was the standard. All of this created vast numbers of tortured souls who, despite the passage of many decades, haunt places that are prime venues for ghost hunters.

Today, the river is spanned by nine bridges, virtually eliminating these social, economic, and transportation barriers. The unification of Eastside and Westside urban centers was further cemented by the location of the Portland International Airport, the Moda Center (home of the Portland Trail Blazers basketball team), and several other cultural attractions on the east side of the Willamette River. Despite the tremendous growth of the city since the 1960s, many unique neighborhoods remain on the east side of Portland where ghost hunters will find old coffeehouses, theatres, bars and restaurants, beautiful parks, and fascinating historic sites. These places with a strong local character provide visitors with different experiences than may be encountered in downtown Portland. Several haunted locations highlight local history, social development, and tragic events that created some very active ghosts. And while you roam the east side of Portland, don't forget to stop by the famous Voodoo Doughnut store at 1501 NE Davis Street.

## GHOST OF THE LONELY MAN

North Portland Library
512 North Killingsworth Street
Portland 97217
503-988-5123
www.multcolib.org/library-location/north-portland

There is no historical record of a death occurring inside the North Portland Library but there is substantial evidence that the building is haunted. The second-floor meeting room, a space that is always kept locked unless a lecture or other gathering is staged, is often visited by a male ghost whose image was first noted on a security monitor. This fellow appears seated in a chair, motionless, as if he were listening to a lecture or waiting for someone. Library staff members spotted him on the monitor and, initially suspecting an intruder, raced upstairs to the meeting room only to find it locked and empty. Often appearing lifelike, the man has been described as thin with gray receding hair, about 50 years old, and wearing a white T-shirt and tan pants. No one on the staff recognizes the man as a regular user of the library or someone from the neighborhood.

It is possible this ghost was one of the workers who built the stately library. In 1912, a Carnegie grant provided funds for construction of this building that included fancy exterior brick designs and vaulted ceilings with massive curved beams anchored by corbels carved with the faces of literary characters or local flora. In addition, some of the ceilings are coffered with huge plaster medallions from which chandeliers hang. After a century of use, the building still looks spectacular and totally different from the bland architecture of libraries constructed since the 1960s. Preservation of its unique style was a prime objective of a major renovation that closed the building for a year. After it reopened on March 21, 2000, ghostly activity on the second floor and on Commercial Street increased significantly.

It has been suggested that the ghost of the North Portland Library may be a visitor from the mortuary that once operated across the street. Reliable sources have reported mysterious footsteps on NE Commercial Street that seem to approach witnesses and pass directly through them. At times, the footfalls are heavy, suggesting that the unseen being is wearing boots. When the pavement is wet, footsteps have been heard crossing Commercial Street, heading toward the library.

It seems likely that at least one spirit whose body was prepared for burial at the Little Chapel of the Chimes may have decided that the library is a more interesting place to linger on the physical plane than a mortuary. After visiting the library, you can investigate the mortuary, since it has been converted to McMenamins Chapel Pub.

*The old North Portland Library may harbor spirits who crossed the street from the former mortuary.*

## GHOST OF THE PIANO MAN

Kaiser Permanente Interstate Medical Office Central
3600 North Interstate Avenue
Portland 97223
503-813-2000

Hospitals are among the most haunted places on the planet. The Central Building at Kaiser Permanente's Interstate campus is no exception. This building houses the oncology library and lab, but I suspect that the ghost that haunts the medical center is linked to the rehabilitation services on the second floor, which include physical and occupational therapy, and the disability assessment clinic. A security guard has reported that many employees at the clinic know of a ghost named Frank who wanders the hallways but moves quickly to the piano in the dining area outside the cafeteria whenever anyone strikes a few keys. Frank does not play the piano, but he is so strongly attracted to it that many suspect he is a former pianist now unable to play because of a stroke or other debilitating illness or injury.

The ghostly image of Frank has been viewed on security cameras. He has been observed walking between the East Building and the Central Building and standing near the piano. Security-staff members suspect that Frank unlocks doors after they are locked. I asked an employee if Frank has demonstrated an affinity for a particular kind of music. She has witnessed his partial apparition several times, regardless of the style of music visitors chose to play. There have been many occasions when Frank shows up simply because the keys have been struck indiscriminately by a visitor who cannot actually play a tune. Frank seems to lose patience with these people and vanishes if children pound on the keys, making a sound that would be irritating to a skilled musician.

## GHOST OF PRIVATE PAUL

The Crow Bar and Miss Delta Restaurant
3954 and 3950 North Mississippi Avenue

Portland 97227
503-280-7099

In 1919, thousands of young men returned from World War I to their homes in Portland still deeply affected by the horrors they had endured while fighting in France. Some had no physical wounds but suffered severely from shellshock, now referred to as post-traumatic stress disorder. Others came home with lungs that were scarred by mustard gas, a new chemical weapon used by the Germans. These soldiers had frequent episodes of airway spasms, similar to asthma, that left them short of breath, starved for air, and drained of energy. In order to help them continue a healing process that was often never completed, several small clinics or rehabilitation facilities were set up in the Portland region. One of those facilities was located on North Mississippi Avenue above a row of storefronts. The apartments were broken up into tiny rooms, each containing two or three beds. A small central kitchen and treatment rooms were located on the first floor. While most soldiers treated at the clinic recovered sufficiently to return to their families or find a place of their own, it is likely that some of them died there. That suspicion seems to be confirmed by the ghostly manifestations of a man dressed as a World War I soldier that occurs in the building.

In the modern apartments on the second floor, residents have witnessed the apparition of a soldier sitting in a rocking chair. Dubbed Private Paul, he appears with considerable detail, including high-top leather boots, an empty gun holster on a belt, and a wide-brimmed hat. The ghost rocks in the chair as he gazes out the window. Witnesses get the distinct impression that his breathing is labored. At times, they hear wheezing and gasping before he vanishes. Private Paul sometimes manifests only by creating a strong gust of air or an intense cold spot.

On the ground floor, patrons of the Crow Bar have reported seeing candles and glasses slide across the bar and wispy apparitions from the corners of their eyes. Women have reported that creepy feeling that a tall person is standing close behind, breathing heavily or wheezing.

Crow Bar staff have had frequent encounters with Private

Paul. Some witnessed bottles falling off the shelves, as if unseen hands were pushing them. In the basement, a chair scoots over the floor, often blocking the path of workers who are moving bar supplies around. This ghost also seems to manifest at the Miss Delta restaurant at 3950 North Mississippi.

Psychics, including myself, who have visited the building confirm that the spirit of a soldier does, indeed, haunt it, moving between the basement and second-floor apartments. Clearly, he suffers from a severe breathing disorder but hopes to make a full recovery. He is probably waiting at the rehabilitation facility for the day when he is able to return home.

## GHOST OF THE OLDEST PROFESSION

White Eagle Saloon & Hotel
836 North Russell Street
Portland 97227
503-282-6810
www.mcmenamins.com/white-eagle-saloon-hotel

Any paranormal expert would probably name the White Eagle as the most haunted place in the Portland area. Constructed in 1899, the two-story, brick building was originally intended to be a respectable café and boardinghouse for the people who labored in the warehouses and factories and on the docks of the industrial side of the Willamette River. For a while, St. Stanislaus, the West Coast's first Polish Catholic church, held their organizational meetings in the building.

By 1905, it had become known as a place that was not safe for polite society. Its owners, Bronislaw Soboleski and William Hryszko, renamed it the White Eagle Saloon and catered to Polish workers who lived and worked in the neighborhood. As industrialization along the riverfront proceeded, bringing with it more bars, brothels, and flophouses, respectable families moved out. They were replaced by a growing number of workers and sailors who stopped at the White Eagle for food, strong drinks, and the services of prostitutes. These services were segregated. On the second floor, 11 small rooms provided space for a busy industry that featured white women. In the basement, black and Asian girls were offered. Supervised by a hulking bouncer, this despicable business went on for years and led to much of the paranormal activity experienced by staff members and astonished patrons of the famous White Eagle Saloon & Hotel. The place is a veritable time capsule for those who take the time to examine numerous architectural features of the first and second floors retained since 1905 and the historical photographs mounted on the wall near the entrance.

The ghost of a bouncer stalks the main floor late at night, usually 30 minutes before closing, looking for unruly customers he intends to throw out onto the sidewalk. Tall and wide, with huge rounded shoulders and a scowl on his face, this tough guy should be taken seriously. He walks from the rear of the bar, near the restrooms, to the front door, pushing aside anyone in his path. Late at night, tired patrons who may have had a long evening don't notice the ethereal hands shoving them out of the narrow aisle, but two people have reported to me that they later discovered palm and finger prints on the skin of their backs.

The bouncer shows up in other locations. Condiments, utensils, and other supplies have flown from the shelves, traveling horizontally for some distance before falling to the floor. Toilet paper in the lady's restroom flies about, toilets flush, and doors swing open before slamming shut. A staff member reported being pushed by large, strong hands as she descended the stairs to the basement. She sustained only minor injuries, but the event was truly frightening. There is no doubt that the bouncer was tough on customers at the White Eagle. One day he failed to show up for work. Days later, rumors began to circulate that he had been drugged and shanghaied, or killed. Perhaps this is the reason he has resumed his duty at the place where his authority was supreme.

The basement is generally off-limits to patrons, but access

*The White Eagle Saloon is an iconic watering hole on the east side of the Willamette River that has stood for more than a century.*

may be granted under special circumstances. It now contains refrigerators, freezers, shelves for storing nonperishables, and an office. Decades ago, flimsy walls divided the space into cells occupied by black and Asian prostitutes. It is believed the girls were kidnapped and kept as sex slaves for paying customers. Some hapless patrons were drugged and shanghaied through a tunnel to the docks. It's no wonder that psychics who enter the space detect sadness and pain. Some sensitives also perceive violence perpetrated on the girls or unruly customers. It seems certain that more than one girl died in the basement, from illness or suicide, and a few patrons also lost their lives to drug and alcohol excess or a beating delivered by the pimps or bouncer. The result is an angry spirit that haunts the place. This ghost opens and closes the freezer doors, causes coins to fall from the ceiling, and touches living persons. It may be responsible for pushing the employee as she descended the stairs.

Another spirit in the White Eagle is believed to be that of Sam Warrick. It has been reported that he was born in one of the second-floor rooms and spent his entire life in the business. As a child, Sam was the gofer and kitchen helper. Later, he tended bar and cleaned up the place. After that, Sam did odd jobs around the saloon to cover his room and board. Sometime in the 1940s, Sam died in one of the hotel rooms. Some of his personal items have been placed in several of the rooms, prompting him to manifest. Passersby on the street have spotted him gazing out the windows. Sleepy hotel guests who have wandered down the hall in the middle of the night to the central restroom have become wide awake when they realized they could see through the haggard old man who stood facing them. Ghost hunters should take a look at historic photos hanging on the walls of the main floor. In some of them, you can see Sam Warrick.

Sam's name has been attached to the legendary ghost story of the White Eagle, but historians are certain he was not the character described as the dapper piano player who fell in love with a second-floor prostitute. The story of Sam and Rose may be little more than urban legend, but given the decades of bar fights, clashes over women, and lives wasted in the place, it does not seem like too much of a stretch. It has been said that Sam desperately wanted to leave the seedy enterprise and miserable neighborhood and take Rose with him. After several months of planning and saving his money, he visited Rose in her room late one December night after her customers had gone home. Hoping to convince her to run away with him that very night, he showed her his wallet packed with money and two train tickets to Seattle. Then he proposed that she leave with him and become his wife.

The legend says that Rose laughed at poor Sam and the ridicule caused him to fly into a rage, smashing her furniture, breaking her mirror, and screaming at her. The bouncer heard the terrible racket and burst into the room just as Sam pulled a pistol from his coat pocket. The two men fought and, although the bouncer was the larger man, Sam broke free of his grasp and shot him. Still in a rage, he shot Rose and then turned the gun on himself.

Many people believe that this murder-suicide created spirits that are responsible for most of the paranormal activity on the second floor. Overnight guests often hear sound bursts of a piano, a woman crying, mirrors shattering, furniture breaking, and the groaning of two men caught in an eternal fight caused by unrequited love.

## GHOSTS OF THE PIONEERS

Lone Fir Cemetery
2115 SE Morrison Street
Portland 97214
503-797-1709
www.oregonmetro.gov/metro-cemeteries

In 1846, when James Stephens buried his father, Emmor, on land owned by Seldon Murray, he had no idea the memorial would eventually be surrounded by the graves of more than 25,000 of Portland's citizens. James and his wife, Elizabeth, ran a ferry service across the Willamette River and never gave any thought to getting into the cemetery business. Even as a few more graves were added to the shady spot now bordered by SE 20th Avenue and SE Stark Street, the place was not formally known as a cemetery. The explosion of the steamship *Gazelle* on the Willamette River in 1854 changed that forever.

On April 8, 1854, at 6:30 A.M., while the ship was tied to a dock, the engineer allowed its steam pressure to rise to dangerous levels. Sensing the imminent disaster, he jumped onto the dock and started running. Ten minutes later, the ship's boilers exploded, killing 21 people instantly. Four others later died of their wounds, while 40 were seriously injured. The large collection of body parts so disturbed local citizens that a decision was made to bury the dead as quickly as possible. Thus 25 graves were opened near that of Emmor Stephens, and locals began to think of the plot of land as a cemetery.

Less than a year later, sensing a good business opportunity, sexton and gravedigger Colburn Barrell purchased 10 acres surrounding the early burial sites and officially established the cemetery. In 1866, Barrell added 20 acres to the enterprise and tried to sell the cemetery to the city of Portland. The offer was declined because the graveyard, sitting east of the Willamette River and reached only by an unreliable ferry and muddy roads, was considered too remote. Noting the compelling name, Lone Fir Cemetery, derived from the solitary tree standing near the original graves, investors Levi Anderson, Robert Pittock, and Byron Cardwell stepped forward and purchased the grounds.

Today, Lone Fir Cemetery is a veritable storehouse of Portland history, containing the remains of 25,000 of the city's famous and infamous citizens in addition to an estimated 10,000 unmarked graves. Among them are the graves of the couple considered to be Lone Fir's founders: James and Elizabeth Stephens. Their monument is an effigy of the couple, standing side by side and facing the tree that inspired the cemetery's name. On the back of their monument is a touching epitaph: *Here we lie by consent, after 57 years 2 months and 2 days sojourning through life awaiting nature's immutable laws to return us back to the elements of the universe, of which we were first composed.*

Lone Fir Cemetery staff members and volunteers offer monthly tours that provide visitors with fascinating histories and explanations of some of the bizarre monuments. They also offer information about paranormal activity known to occur in this beautiful place. In October, the Friends of Lone Fir Cemetery stage a Halloween tour called "Untimely Departures," which highlights the graveyard's paranormal legacy.

Most people who stroll through this cemetery feel something odd. Sometimes it is simply the play of shadows and wind, but others have reported passing through the gate and immediately becoming aware of an inexplicable change in atmosphere. On warm days, it is common for visitors to step into a column of air that is so cold that they start to shiver and pull a jacket over their shoulders. At several graves, visitors get a feeling that they should not stand close to the headstone or monument. Some have reported feeling pushed away or hitting an invisible wall. At times, voices fill the heads of astonished and frightened witnesses.

One portion of the cemetery in particular creates eerie sensations. In 1858, Dr. James C. Hawthorne (1818-91) established a private insane asylum supported by Multnomah County. Over the years, hundreds of patients died while under his supervision. Often, the deceased had no immediate family willing to take charge of the remains, so Dr. Hawthorne buried them in unmarked graves in a section of Lone Fir Cemetery now known as Hawthorne's Plot. The remains of 132 patients have been discovered through excavation, but it is likely that many more lie hidden beneath the green sod. Upon his death, Dr. Hawthorne was buried near his patients in the southeast portion of the cemetery.

Block 14 is also a site of intense and frequent paranormal activity, attributed to an unknown number of Chinese who were buried there. In 1956, the county exhumed several bodies and relocated them, with the assumption that all of the unfortunate deceased persons had been accounted for. In 2000, excavation for a new building turned up more remains, bringing construction to a halt. At this site, sensitive visitors feel as though they are being pulled downward by unseen hands. Sound bursts in Mandarin are frequent, and ghost hunters often feel as though they are pushed aside.

More than 250 Civil War veterans are buried here, in addition to several notables from Portland's past:

**Colburn Barrell:** He descended from *Mayflower* pilgrims and sailed with Captain Gray on a trade voyage that discovered the Columbia River. Barrell owned the steamship *Gazelle* which exploded, sending 25 souls to this cemetery. Block 1/Lot 1/Grave 2N.

**Cornelius Beal:** He was a divorce attorney from the early days. Block 18/Lot 5A/Grave 3S.

**William Beck:** He was a pioneer gun merchant and advocate for the first bridge over the Willamette River (Morrison). Block 1/Lot 47/Grave 3S.

**Angeline Berry:** She founded the Humane Society, Good Samaritan Hospital, and YWCA and donated land for Grace Episcopal Church. Block 8/Lot 46/Grave 2N.

**Crawford Dobbins:** He died in the *Gazelle* explosion. His burial led to the formal declaration of the grounds as a cemetery. Block 1/Lot 1/Grave 2S.

**Dr. James C. Hawthorne:** He ran the Oregon Asylum for the Insane/Moral Treatment at the end of the Oregon Trail. He buried 132 inmates at Lone Fir. Block 8M/Lot 44/Grave 1N.

**Asa Lovejoy:** He founded Portland but lost the coin toss that named it. He established Oregon's first telegraph company, Oregon City Woolen Mills, and Portland's first Masonic Lodge. Block 8M/Lot 50/Grave 2N.

**Esther Lovejoy:** This "Doctor to the World" was a suffragette, the first female director of the city's Health Department, and the first director of the Medical Women's International Association. Block 34.

**Donald MacLeay:** This Scottish businessman worked in banking; raising wheat, lumber, and salmon; and shipping. He invested his profits in Portland's growth, and his family donated MacLeay Park to the city. Block 17/Lot 3/Mausoleum.

**Martha MacLeay:** She was married to Donald for seven years and had four children. She was known as a progressive philanthropist. Block 17/Lot 3/Mausoleum.

**Robert Pittock:** This brother of Henry Pittock was a grocer. Block 1/Lot 37/Grave 2S.

**Earl Riley:** He was a colorful but corrupt mayor. His father built the original Canyon Road. Block 8/Lot 47/Grave 2S.

**Dr. William Royal:** This Civil War doctor was infamous as a captain who allegedly shanghaied his own son. Block 13/Lot 12/Grave 3N.

**William Warren:** He is one of over 250 Civil War burials in Lone Fir Cemetery. Block 1/Lot 52/Grave 1N.

**Capt. Daniel Wright:** He went to California for the Gold Rush and used some of his money to purchase a beautiful spot in the cemetery. Block 4/Lot 70/Grave 3N.

*The Macleay family mausoleum is the tallest monument in Lone Fir Cemetery and a gathering place for ghost hunters and ghosts.*

## THEATRICAL GHOSTS

Bagdad Theater
3702 SE Hawthorne Boulevard
Portland 97214
503-236-9234
www.mcmenamins.com/219-bagdad-theater-pub-home

There are good reasons why old theatres are ranked in the top five places to experience paranormal phenomena. Theatres that have stood for many decades have invariably soaked up intense emotions and energy from members of the audience, dancers, singers, musicians, actors, comedians, directors, producers, and even stagehands and retained them in the walls, chandeliers, stage, seats, and dressing rooms. These residuals or imprints of emotions and energy often "play," creating sound bursts of past performances that may include a voice speaking lines or singing, the applause of an audience, or cues shouted by a director. Residuals may also include the sound of musical instruments, flashes of light, and apparitions of performers, members of an audience, and stagehands who may have fallen from a catwalk only to die onstage. People who work in these old theatres and patrons who attend screenings of modern movies, rock concerts, or comedy performances are often astonished when they encounter the apparition of an actor, musician, or member of an audience dressed in clothing from a long-bygone era. This is no surprise to ghost hunters, however, because nearly all old theatres are haunted. After death, performers, directors, conductors, and stagehands often chose to stay at the site of their greatest accomplishments, awaiting the applause of an adoring audience. Often, ghostly members of an audience remain as well, hoping to see an actor or actress with whom they have fallen in love.

The old Bagdad Theater has all the elements to make it a haunted venue despite renovation into a modern movie house, pub, and private party rooms. First-run films, a huge screen, 20,000-watt surround sound, a digital projector, "rocker" seating, and first-rate food and drink concessions haven't diminished the imprints and ghostly activity that may be experienced at this fascinating theatre.

The Bagdad opened in 1927, on the very cusp of the commercialization of talking pictures. The $100,000 construction budget was huge for the day, allowing architects and builders to create a spectacular entertainment venue that included a Middle Eastern motif, a grand fountain, a colonnade hundreds of feet long, red-tile hoods above the windows, decorative molding, rafters, arched doorways, and wrought-iron balconets and lighting features. Carrying the Middle Eastern theme to the extreme, usherettes wore uniforms described as "Arabian style."

Declared by Mayor George Baker at the time to be a "triumph of artistry and craftsmanship," the place was spectacular and immediately became known as the foremost entertainment venue on the east side of Portland. Talking movies and vaudeville attracted the first patrons, but the Bagdad's popularity continued through the 1950s with first-run movies and live stage performances by renowned entertainers such as Sammy Davis, Jr. In the 1970s, the Bagdad hosted the Oregon premiere of *One Flew Over the Cuckoo's Nest*. Upon joining the McMenamins restaurant and entertainment group, the theatre underwent extensive renovation, with great care taken to preserve its original character.

Is this fascinating theatre haunted? Yes, it remains a literal hotbed of paranormal activity, but none of it is frightening or threatening to those who are fortunate enough to encounter a ghost or experience the replay of an imprint from the 1930s.

For many years, the apparition of a male figure has been spotted walking about the upstairs lobby. At times, this apparition is so lifelike that witnesses have been able to see the wide lapels of his jacket, his shiny bowtie, and his slicked-back hair. This ghost moves around as if he is on duty and charged with making sure theatre guests are having a good time. He shows up most often when a patron spills a drink, bumps into a chair, or collides with another guest.

A female ghost manifests in various seats of the last two

*The old Bagdad Theater offers patrons modern amenities, but it retains its 1920s character as well as several ghosts from that era.*

rows. It seems clear that this woman was an ardent fan of a man who was a regular performer at the Bagdad Theater. She may have fallen in love with his singing voice or dramatic delivery, or simply watched one movie after another for many years, silently wishing she had become an actress. This ghost appears to be wearing a small hat that was stylish in the 1940s and a fur draped over her shoulders.

Patrons who are not fortunate enough to witness these ghosts may encounter unexplained gusts of wind, cold spots, and the dimming of lights. In the restrooms, doors to the stalls often vibrate as if a ghost desperately needs to gain entry but cannot generate the energy to open the door fully. In addition, balls of light often flash in front of the screen before a movie starts and then move up and down the aisles.

## MYSTERIOUS LADIES OF THE LAKE

Laurelhurst Park
SE Cesar E. Chavez Boulevard at Stark Street
Portland 97255
503-823-2525

In most of the cities where I've conducted paranormal investigations, I've encountered stories of a female ghost that appears in or near an urban lake or pond where she allegedly drowned by accident, suicide, or murder. With very few exceptions, no historical record or other documentation could be found to support the legend. In a few cases, witness reports of a ghostly image are so frequent and similar that paranormal investigators concede there may be some truth to the supposition that a woman did, indeed, die in the lake and that she haunts the location of her death. It is quite unusual, however, that we have a name, date, and other evidence that verifies the death while pointing to suspicious circumstances that may serve as a basis of the haunting.

Ten-year-old Donald West played at Laurelhurst Park so often that he knew every spot at the edge of the lake that would allow him to get close to the ducks or drop a fishing line in the cloudy water. Close to noon on October 9, 1936, while making his usual stroll around the lake searching for dead fish and ducks, Donald spotted something unusual. He found a woman's shoe and coat resting on the mud of a tiny inlet. Donald immediately notified park watchman E. J. Dahl. Dahl's initial notion was that someone went swimming in the lake and, dripping wet and cold, raced to a nearby car, leaving some clothing behind. In the pocket of the coat, however, he found some cash and $300 in traveler's checks. He also found material indicating the coat belonged to Alla Warineth, aged 45, of Spokane, Washington. Pondering the significance of this discovery, Dahl looked out over the cloudy surface of the lake only to see Alla floating face down. Later, police and firefighters recovered her body, and the coroner concluded that the death was a suicide. A search of the entire park failed to turn up other articles of clothing, an abandoned car, or other evidence that might explain how or why Alla had traveled from Spokane to this idyllic park in Portland.

Alla Warineth might have been forgotten if it weren't for another unusual discovery that occurred many years later. While jogging the perimeter of the lake one morning, a man spotted a woman standing at the edge of the water, hands clasped and head bowed as if in prayer. Moments after passing her, he heard a splash that seemed to echo through the cold, damp air. Retracing his steps, the man saw her about 20 yards from shore, floating face down. He jumped into the lake and attempted to reach her. Stroking through the algae-choked water, he found that as he came within a few feet of the floating, motionless body, it seemed to move farther away. As his rescue efforts continued, he became chilled and extremely frustrated that he could not reach the woman. Finally, with cramping muscles and gasping breaths, he made one last attempt, only to watch the body disappear before his eyes. The man was certain she did not slip beneath the surface but clearly vanished as if she were never there.

Soon after this story circulated around the neighborhood, others came forward to report a woman suddenly appearing, either floating on the lake or standing at the water's edge, then vanishing. So far, no one has reported intelligent interaction with this woman, so we cannot conclude that witnesses have actually seen the ghost of Alla Warineth. The images seen by many people may be residuals or imprints of the tragic event that were triggered to "play" by specific environmental conditions or the sensitivities of witnesses.

It is possible that the ghostly image of a woman floating on the lake is not that of Alla Warineth. On February 25, 2008, the body of another woman, 37-year-old Heidi Anderson, was found in the lake at Laurelhurst Park. She had been missing since February 8. A hiker had discovered Heidi's hat, coat, cellphone, and wallet under a shrub. The wallet, which contained money, the presence of the cellphone, and the neatly folded clothing suggested to police that the tragedy was not the result of a robbery. In fact, nothing at the scene raised suspicions of an assault, and the autopsy found no evidence of a crime. Family, friends, and co-workers reported to police that Heidi had had no problems with drugs, alcohol, or mental health. On February 8, the last day she was seen alive, however, she reportedly got out of a friend's car after the sudden onset of paranoia. She then boarded a bus but got off after traveling for only one minute. Within hours, a missing person's report was filed and a search initiated at the corner of 90th Street and Sandy Boulevard, the last place Heidi was seen alive. More than two weeks later, the search ended with the discovery of her body in Laurelhurst Park.

Paranormal investigators who visit Laurelhurst Park should conduct EVP sweeps in an attempt to capture a female voice that may respond when the names Alla and Heidi are spoken. Also, imaging devices should be used to obtain characteristics

*The calm waters of the lake and peaceful atmosphere of Laurelhurst Park enable psychics to experience the presence of two women who committed suicide there.*

of the ghostly woman seen here. Pictures of Alla cannot be found online, but several photos of Heidi are available.

## PARANORMAL CSI

Fatalities in Tragic Car Collision
SE Gladstone Street at SE 28th Place
Portland 97202

At this scene of a horrific two-car accident in 2013, offerings are often found attached to a utility pole, assuring the deceased that they are not forgotten. Friends and neighbors pin notes or crosses, leave flowers, or light a candle to honor the memory and mourn the loss of Paul Lawrence Knepper, aged 55, and his 90-year-old mother, Hazel Agnes Knepper. These mementoes may have something to do with the paranormal remnants of this event that sensitives perceive as they walk the path of the Kneppers' car after it was crushed by a speeding SUV and thrown against the utility pole, killing Paul and Hazel.

Daniel Troy Johnson, aged 29, spent much of the afternoon of March 9, 2013, drinking with friends. A few minutes before five o'clock, he jumped behind the wheel of his Cadillac Escalade, with three pals and a dog taking the remaining seats. Fully inebriated and joking with his friends, Johnson sped north on 28th Place. According to witnesses and the police investigation, he was traveling far in excess of the posted speed limit. At the intersection with SE Gladstone Street, Johnson ran the stop sign, slamming into the passenger side of a Toyota Corolla driven by Paul Knepper. Hazel, sitting in the front passenger seat, was probably killed instantly by the impact. It threw the Toyota across the intersection into a utility pole on the northeast corner, severely injuring Paul. Moments later, as shocked residents tried to render aid to the injured man, he died.

This horrible tragedy was made even more reprehensible by Johnson's escape from the scene. Leaving a friend and the dog injured in the car, he and the two others extricated themselves from the wrecked vehicle and ran. Johnson was captured a short time later and charged with two counts of manslaughter in the second degree, felony hit and run, assault in the fourth degree, and DUI. He was sentenced to 18 years in prison.

What remains at this location that may be paranormal? Sensitives who walk the path of the Kneppers' car perceive an imprint, or residual, of the horrible impact. Some actually perceive the sound of two vehicles colliding, which, at the time of the accident, was heard blocks away. At the utility pole, a female presence has been detected. This woman is terribly sad and seems confused and in need of help. Some ghost hunters have speculated that this is the ghost of Hazel Knepper mourning the loss of her son, Paul. Only a few weeks earlier, Hazel had lost another son, John, to cancer. It is also possible that the female presence at this site is an imprint of intense emotions experienced by a horrified resident who raced from her house to the scene hoping to save one of the victims.

## GHOSTS OF THE POOR FARM

Edgefield
2126 SW Halsey Street
Troutdale 97060
503-669-8610
www.mcmenamins.com/edgefield

After decades of operating under deplorable conditions, the county's first poor farm, Hillside Farm, located in Portland's West Hills, was shut down in 1911 and its 211 inmates were transferred to a new facility in Troutdale. Located 16 miles from the heart of Portland, it was within reach of county administrators and sheriff's deputies but far enough away that the derelicts it housed would not trouble affluent citizens. Despite its purpose, the place was constructed in a grand style that included fancy brickwork on the exterior, spacious hallways with intricate woodwork, large dining rooms, recreation rooms, an infirmary, library, and facilities for teaching inmates crafts and skills they might use to regain a productive lifestyle. In addition, several outbuildings were erected to support farming operations. Edgefield was constructed to house vagrants, but many of its inmates were skilled or educated people who had simply had a run of bad luck due to illness or injury. During its 71 years of operation, however, the place also housed emotionally disturbed children, adults with mental illness, alcoholics, addicts, tuberculosis patients, released prisoners who had no means or support to live a law-abiding life, the blind, deaf persons, and anyone deemed to be a social deviant.

Despite this seemingly deprecating description of Edgefield's inmates, those who worked the farm created a hugely successful enterprise. Inmates provided themselves and the staff with all of the fruit, vegetables, dairy, pork products, and poultry they needed. In some years, they produced a surplus of food, which was sent to the county's hospitals and jails.

During the Great Depression, Edgefield's population grew to more than 600 residents. With the onset of World War II, greater opportunities for employment reduced the population to about 200. However, many inmates who entered Edgefield in the 1930s were never able to leave. As the residents grew older, portions of the facility were converted to a nursing home. Undoubtedly, several inmates died here, and there are rumors that many bodies were buried on the grounds.

By 1972, other social programs to assist the indigent made Edgefield obsolete. Still, the last patient did not depart the old home until 1982. Suffering attacks by vandals and abuse by the homeless, the vacant facility faced demolition by the county. Fortunately, the Troutdale Historical Society stepped in and mounted a campaign to save it. Several prospective buyers passed on the development opportunities until the McMenamin brothers saw its great potential and invested the time and money to make Edgefield the spectacular resort that it is today. With a theatre, winery, brewpub, indoor and outdoor dining, comfortable overnight accommodations, and beautiful gardens, Edgefield is an ideal destination for visitors to the Portland region.

*Edgefield started as a poor farm but now offers guests a full range of services, including a chance to encounter ghosts.*

If you are looking for ghosts, this place may be the most haunted hotel in Oregon. In fact, a log is kept at the front desk in which guests may record their paranormal experiences at the old poor farm. The log indicates that room 215 is one of the most active paranormal sites, although many entries suggest that the entire second floor is haunted. The third floor, the winery, the Black Rabbit Bar, rooms that once housed the infirmary, the old power station, and the Distillery Bar have ghosts as well. Guests who have slept in room 215 have had encounters with a "spirit dog" that licks their feet or touches their face with its cold nose. A short, elderly woman has also been spotted shuffling across this room with an unsteady gait. In several rooms, guests have left personal items on a bed or table while they were out. When they returned, some items were missing or rearranged in patterns.

A woman dressed as a nurse has been spotted walking the hallways in broad daylight. Other females dressed as inmates wander the corridors, show up in the women's restrooms, and

*Paintings and other architectural features enable ghost hunters to get in touch with an earlier era that produced hundreds of imprints and ghosts.*

glide up and down the stairs. A little girl descends the front stairs and walks toward the parking lot but vanishes after passing the fountain. Some of the female ghosts serenade guests with hymns or recite nursery rhymes.

The Power Station Pub was once Edgefield's power plant and laundry. Today, the popular eatery is haunted. Staff members have said they often feel a presence in the room that hovers close by and creates that creepy feeling of being watched. In the Black Rabbit Bar, some staff members have encountered an angry ghost, but this spirit does not harm the living.

I could not find any credible reports of abuse of inmates by poor-farm staff members or attacks on an inmate by other residents. A housekeeper told me she had heard that a girl had been murdered in the old laundry (now the Power Station Pub), but I found no corroboration in historical records. Given the high probability that many inmates were mentally unstable and, perhaps, prone to violence, I would not be surprised if unnatural deaths occurred at the old poor farm. Some sensitive visitors have encountered intense cold spots and places where strong negative energy creates perceptions of fear, rage, and pain. Several guests have heard unexplained sobbing, crying, and screams and called the front desk to report their impression that someone was in distress. The most fascinating thing about the paranormal activity at Edgefield is that much of it occurs in daylight hours. If you want the full-blown paranormal experience, however, plan to spend at least one night.

## CHAPTER 4

# Vancouver and North Portland

North Portland, Oregon, and Vancouver, Washington, are distinct political entities but they have many economic, social, cultural, and historical ties that, in several ways, unite them as a single community. The two major bridges that cross the mighty Columbia River make travel between Vancouver and Portland easy for commuters and others who wish to enjoy countless opportunities for shopping, recreation, entertainment, education, and sporting events. As early as 1846, Dr. John McLoughlin, superintendent of the Columbia District of the Hudson's Bay Company at Fort Vancouver, realized that the region comprised a unique place. Perhaps it was this idea that prompted him to found a city in Oregon and support the American annexation of Oregon Territory, which included land that would someday be Washington State.

Visitors who arrive at Portland's International Airport will find that they can, in a few minutes, cross the Columbia and begin their ghost investigations at historic Fort Vancouver and Vancouver Barracks, where the ideas of a city on the Willamette and the beautiful state of Oregon were first conceived. Stops at modern entities such as a fast-food restaurant, park, deadly intersection, and historic house that has become a farmers market will keep you grounded in the 21st century, but always be on the lookout for fascinating ghosts who lived during the early history of this region.

## MURDER OF ANNA SVIDERSKY

McDonald's Restaurant
2814 NE Andresen Road

Vancouver, WA 98661
360-693-8481

Late in the afternoon of April 20, 2006, schizophrenic sex offender David Barton Sullivan grew increasingly captivated with the idea of violence. He would later admit that his greatest desire was to "hurt a female." Described as a level-two registered sex offender with a criminal history that included an assault in 2001 and incarceration in a state facility for mental illness, Sullivan was not under the supervision of social workers or law-enforcement officials when he decided to kill.

After sunset, Sullivan walked alongside busy Andresen Road for several minutes before deciding that he would find a victim inside the McDonald's restaurant. With a long kitchen knife concealed by his coat, he entered and spotted Anna Esther Svidersky.

Born in the Soviet Union in 1998, Anna immigrated to the U.S. as an infant and grew up to be a typical Western teenager. Eager to fulfill her American dream, she worked three jobs during her senior year at Fort Vancouver High School. Her goal of going to college may have been on her mind as she worked at McDonald's, unaware that her murderer had entered the building and was walking straight toward her. According to witnesses, the attack was brief. Sullivan pulled the knife from his coat and stabbed Anna in the chest with a single, strong thrust. Covered with blood, he ran from the restaurant as Anna fell to the floor. She died a short time later at a local hospital.

As Sullivan ran down the street, he dropped the knife. Several patrons of the restaurant ran after him as police rushed to the scene with a canine unit. Moments later, Sullivan was surrounded and taken into custody. On June 26, 2007, Sullivan was acquitted by reason of insanity. He now resides in a mental hospital.

It is difficult to enter this McDonald's restaurant without feeling the negative energy that remains there. In particular, the table for two near the half-wall dividing the dining area from the counter, where Anna was stabbed, still harbors an atmosphere of mental chaos and pain. Does the ghost of

Anna Svidersky haunt this place? I was unable to capture any evidence that the 17-year-old girl was still there, but there is undoubtedly an intense, paranormal residual of her murder that sensitives can easily detect.

Aside from imprints, and possibly ghostly manifestations, there is something quite unique and paranormal at this location. When the story of Anna's murder poured through news and Internet outlets, people all over the world became captivated by her biography, the dreams she pursed, and the tragedy of her death. The newly emerging world of social media was filled with messages of condolence and testimony of Anna's passion and kindness. The British newspaper *The Guardian* compared the widespread interest and outpouring of emotion to the world's reaction to the death of Princess Diana in 1997.

This unusual response to the death of an otherwise obscure American teenager was due, in part, to the nearly immediate dissemination of bad news around the world. In addition, Stephen Coleman, professor of political communication at Leeds University, explained that the tragedy touched young people deeply because of the concept of "shared space" fostered by social networks. The news made many people feel vulnerable and frightened and, thus, created a confluence of emotions almost simultaneously. An interesting form of mass empathy—grief over the death of a stranger—created an emotional energy in millions of people worldwide that became focused on that McDonald's restaurant on Andresen Road in Vancouver, Washington. The result is a kind of nexus that may give us a paranormal experience of fear and sadness in a busy fast-food restaurant.

## DOUBLE MURDER IN "DARK PARK"

David Douglas Park
1016 North Garrison Road
Vancouver, WA 98664
360-487-8311
www.cityofvancouver.us/parksrec/page/david-douglas-park

This park was named for Fort Vancouver botanist and scholar David Douglas (1799-1834), who distinguished himself by identifying hundreds of species of plants indigenous to the American Northwest that were unknown in Europe, but few people remember the man or his role in discovering the natural treasures of the Portland area. In fact, since 1989, David Douglas Park has been known as "Dark Park" due to a horrific double murder that occurred there. The details of this tragic event are well known because the perpetrator kept a diary of his actions that included his speculation of ways he might improve his techniques for kidnapping, rape, and murder. Be aware that the details of this grisly double murder will be quite disturbing. Ghost hunters who visit this area can perform investigations with a few essential facts, however.

Early in the evening of Monday, September 4, 1989, 11-year-old Cole Neer and his 10-year-old brother, Billy, raced their bikes through the wooded area of David Douglas Park, anxious to get home for dinner. They found the dirt path blocked by a young man, Westley Allan Dodd (1961-93). Instantly achieving control over the boys, he ordered them to leave their bikes in the brush and walk with him. Finding a secluded spot far from the ball fields, Dodd tied the boys' hands, molested them, and then stabbed them with a crude knife. According to Dodd, all of this occurred while the boys cried and begged to be allowed to go home.

Barely alive, Billy was found at the edge of the woods near Topeka Lane. He died an hour later at a local hospital. Police initially believed that the crime involved only one victim but soon learned that Cole was missing. At two o'clock Tuesday morning, Cole's lifeless, bloody body was found.

Knowing the tragic story of Cole and Billy Neer, it is impossible to walk the wooded area of this park without feeling the energy of their horrific ordeal. For me, the experience becomes deeply depressing when I recall that the frightened little boys repeatedly asked their molester, "Will it hurt?" and "When can I go home?"

Sensitives who walk the shaded trails of the park will hear

the laughter of two boys. These are not sounds carried on the wind from the distant ball fields but rather joyful sounds that seem to move past astonished visitors, starting quietly, getting louder as they pass by, then becoming soft and distant again. Psychics get the impression that the Neer boys are reliving a happy moment in their lives, riding their bikes through the beautiful, mysterious forest as they head home for dinner. I truly hope that is what they are doing. Standing amid the shadows of this park, I can shake myself out of my empathic awareness of their pain and agony only by focusing on a moment of joy experienced by these little ghosts.

## OLD CITY CEMETERY IN VANCOUVER

Mill Plain Boulevard at Grand Boulevard
Vancouver, WA 98661
360-693-1562
www.cityofvancouver.us/publicworks/page/city-cemeteries

Contrary to popular opinion, cemeteries are rarely haunted by the ghosts of people interred under fancy monuments or in elaborate mausoleums. The vast majority of ghosts prefer to reside in a place that was important to them when they were alive. Homes, businesses, boats, and even airplanes are far more attractive places than a grave, and they offer emotional stability, a sense of familiarity, and opportunities to stay close to loved ones. No matter how ornate a headstone may be, a graveyard is not the kind of place that could entice a ghost to take up spiritual residence. Certainly, there are instances when a ghost becomes attached to a cemetery, but it is rare for even large graveyards to harbor more than a few ghosts. Cemeteries, however, are covered with imprints created by the emotions of grieving family members. This is certainly true of the Old City Cemetery in Vancouver.

Family members who may have visited a grave several times a year for decades could easily create intense imprints

*Orbs often have no validity as evidence of the paranormal, but when they occur in a cemetery they may signal a ghostly presence.*

of emotions that remain intact and quite strong for a century or more. Each grave may have several imprints, creating a veritable mantle of paranormal energy that can be detected with audio recorders, EMF detectors, infrared imaging, and psychic sensitivities.

Opened in 1867, the Old City Cemetery currently contains about 650 monuments, but local historians believe that more than 1,000 bodies are buried there. Some of the dead worked for the famous Hudson's Bay Company at nearby Fort Vancouver. Later additions were pioneers who traveled West on the Oregon Trail. Despite the noisy traffic on Mill Plain Boulevard, the cemetery has a creepy ambience almost any time of day. Tall trees cast long shadows and keep the air cool, giving the place a chilly atmosphere.

Look for the grave of Arthur Haine. Kicked out of New York by his family after a torrid affair with a showgirl, he arrived in Vancouver in 1871 and became prominent in the town's society. Never far from scandal, Haine became even more famous by arranging his own funeral, which included a brass band. En route to the City Cemetery, his casket slipped off the wagon, giving onlookers a last look at the rather pale gentleman.

The best places to find intense imprints in this cemetery are at the graves of children. If you seek ghosts, look for damaged or vandalized headstones. Ghosts tend to know if a monument is damaged, and they become quite active as they seek the attention of anyone who might make repairs.

If you are visiting Vancouver near Halloween, join the cemetery tour to learn about pious and scandalous citizens who are buried here. Reenactors portray the dead, adding entertaining and macabre elements to your visit.

## HIGH AND DANGEROUS

100 Block of SE Columbia Way
At intersection with freeway off-ramp
Vancouver, WA 98661

On Sunday, November 17, 2013, after hours of drinking and smoking marijuana, Ian Cole put on a deadly demonstration of reckless driving on Columbia House Boulevard. According to witnesses, he drove his 2003 Ford Mustang both east and west on the road, swerving around other cars at a high rate of speed. Apparently, he was trying to entertain his three passengers. At one point, he performed 360s at the intersection of Columbia House Boulevard and Columbia Way. Approaching the corner where the freeway off-ramp joins Columbia Way, he lost control of the car and hit a power pole and transformer box.

Cole staggered from the vehicle and wandered away to call for a friend to pick him up. With a blood-alcohol level of 0.97, he admitted to being "buzzed" and feeling "slow, relaxed, and mellow" from the marijuana. He was so high that he ignored his passengers. Inside the car, his friend, Jesse Orellano-Leister, 20, was dead, while Maxwell Borders, 19, and Benjamin Folk, 25, were unconscious and seriously injured. Folk later died at a local hospital. Cole was arrested and tried for vehicular homicide while driving under the influence, hit and run resulting in injury, and hit and run resulting in death. After learning of the deaths of Folk and Orellano-Leister, and recognizing his culpability, Cole stated, "Suicide doesn't sound like a bad idea."

What remains at the scene today? I discovered some fascinating imprints and a ghost. The atmosphere surrounding the power pole is dense, and there is a sensation of being pulled downward, as if gravity is stronger at this site. Sensitives also hear an audio imprint of a crash. A ghost, confused and in pain, wanders about but stays close to the power pole. I captured an EVP of a man sobbing at this location.

## GHOST OF THE CHILDLESS MATRON

Historic Slocum House
605 Esther Street
Vancouver, WA 98660-3021
360-737-8298

From 1966 to 2012, the Slocum House was a popular boutique theatre seating 65 patrons in an intimate setting. With six to eight shows a season and more than 160 season ticketholders, the theatre was well supported and recognized by many as a centerpiece of a revitalized neighborhood. Its creative atmosphere attracted a number of spirits, including the ghost of Laura Slocum (1838-1914). I've included old theatres on my list of the top five places to find ghosts, so it's no wonder that this marvelous place is haunted.

After achieving success as a merchant, Charles Slocum (1834-1912) started construction of this Italianate-style home in 1867 about one block from its current location. In 1966, the house was moved to make way for a redevelopment project.

Reportedly, Laura could not have children, but she enjoyed inviting neighborhood kids into the house for cookies, and she sometimes hosted parties for them. Her affinity for children may explain the frequent appearance of a cloudlike apparition when children's plays or parties were later held in the building. Witnesses described the apparition as being humanoid while revealing very little detail. Many feel that it was a female spirit,

*Charles and Laura Slocum built this large house and hosted parties here for children of the neighborhood.*

most likely that of Laura Slocum. This apparition appears at several places within the house, most often in the space used as a theatre.

Writer Jeff Davis recounted the experiences of a caretaker who encountered a menacing presence in the basement. While searching for costume items, she caught movement at the periphery of her vision. At one point, she spotted a humanoid figure that quickly faded away, leaving only a growing feeling that the spirit was malevolent or, at the very least, upset that a human had invaded its private space. This ghost may be the spirit of Charles Slocum. Reportedly, he was not as fond of children as his wife. During theatre productions for children, a male presence was frequently noted moving about among patrons, creating annoying sounds while generating negative energy. He was known to stand at the rear of the theatre and laugh or cough. Apparently, he left an indelible mark on seats B-6 and 7, because patrons often reported extreme discomfort in those seats and moved, leaving them empty for many performances.

In 2012, the Slocum House was investigated by the cast members of *Dead Files*, psychic Amy Allan and retired police detective Steve DiShiavi (episode 2.4, "Final Curtain Call"). Amy discovered a male spirit she described as "seven feet tall and broad" who was annoyed with living persons in the house. Steve interviewed several staff members of the theatre, all of whom had paranormal experiences with the Slocums.

It is possible that the menacing ghost of the Slocum House is actually that of Amos Short, who died in 1853 at sea while returning to Vancouver from San Francisco. Amos and Esther Short had owned the land on which the Slocum House came to rest in 1966. By 1848, the Shorts had built a cabin and established a profitable farm at the site. By 1850, disputes with the British led to a gunfight in which Amos shot and killed two men at a place now known as Esther Short Park. The ghost of feisty Amos Short may still be on guard, protecting the property on which the Slocum House now sits.

The Slocum House is now home to the Vancouver Farmers Market.

*Orbs on the stairs may signal a spiritual presence of Charles Slocum or Amos Short.*

## GHOSTS OF THE PALLBEARERS

Providence Academy
400 East Evergreen Boulevard #105
Vancouver, WA 98660
360-694-3271
www.thehistorictrust.org/providence-academy

This magnificent building resembles the great Georgian halls I've investigated on the East Coast. Constructed in 1871 by the Sisters of Providence and opened as the House of Providence in 1873, it boasts brick walls, balconies, ornately framed windows, and a tall cupola that stand in stark contrast to nearby modern buildings. The architecture and the impression of antiquity it evokes also raise suspicions of ghosts.

The stately building served as a boarding school for girls from 1873 until shortly after World War II, when it accepted boys and discontinued housing. After the school closed in 1966, the rooms were reconfigured into a café, studio, gallery, and office space, and the beautiful chapel was restored to its 19th-century grandeur. The chapel may be the most haunted place in the Academy.

From 1890 to 1950, funerals and memorial services were staged in the chapel for military personnel from Vancouver Barracks. Naturally, many of these ceremonies were somber affairs complete with grieving survivors, comrades-in-arms, and officers decked out in ribbons and medals. In every case, the casket containing the deceased was carried slowly into the chapel and afforded all the honors the military could muster. Often the pallbearers were soldiers who performed that duty as part of their day-to-day service. One of those soldiers seems to be on the job to this day, floating down the center aisle of the chapel in a lock-step fashion, his blue jacket and its brass decorations clearly apparent to sensitive witnesses. On some occasions, more than one pallbearer has been spotted. After sitting quietly in the chapel for several minutes, I caught the transparent, partial image of at least four soldiers in formal uniform. They appeared halfway down the aisle, moving slowly toward the sanctuary. As they approached the steps, they vanished.

*Standing tall and stately, the Academy hosts the ghosts and imprints of several funerals.*

Other writers have reported sightings of children in the hallways of the building and on the stairs. At times they pass quietly, but there are reports of disembodied laughter flashing down the corridor. The ghost of a housekeeper who supposedly had a heart attack on the stairs may also haunt the Academy. This ghost appears to be wearing a long gray skirt partly covered by a soiled apron. A restroom near the café is haunted by the spirit of an angry girl who casts a discomforting stare at women who enter alone.

## VANCOUVER BARRACKS

Fort Vancouver National Historic Site
612 East Reserve Street
Vancouver, WA 98661
360-816-6230
www.nps.gov/fova

Despite its location in the state of Washington, on the north shore of the Columbia River, Fort Vancouver has close historical, social, economic, and even political links with Oregon and the city of Portland that provide a basis for research of paranormal phenomena anywhere in the region. Founded in 1825 as a fur-trading center and Western headquarters of the Hudson's Bay Company, the fort initially housed military personnel and explorers but later became a destination for immigrants moving westward along the famed Oregon Trail. In the Great Migration of 1843, as many as 1,000 Americans arrived at the fort before moving on to homesteads throughout the territory. After an arduous five-month trek on the Oregon Trail, many of the people who would later develop the city of Portland found much-needed refuge at the fort, facilities for repair of wagons, and stock to replace their draft animals. Without that assistance, Oregon and the Rose City may have grown very differently from what we know today.

During the 21 years that he served as Fort Vancouver's

first manager, Dr. John McLoughlin, a subject of the British Crown, was a beneficent supporter of American immigration into Oregon Territory. While maintaining peaceful relations between the American and British, he also dealt fairly with local Indians by promoting lucrative trade. In 1846, McLoughlin retired and moved south to a beautiful spot on the Willamette River where he founded Oregon City. There, he promoted the political organization of Oregon Territory, which would ultimately lead to statehood in 1859. Known today as the "Father of Oregon," he built a home that still stands in Oregon City and attracts tourists and ghost hunters. His legacy at Fort Vancouver is represented by a full-scale replica of the military and trade facilities he founded in 1825.

Nothing of the original Fort Vancouver remains today aside from artifacts recovered through archeological digs. The fort replica, comprised of 10 buildings and a 10-foot-tall log fence, includes a museum that contains more than 2 million objects found in the excavations. This fascinating historic site is not a venue targeted by ghost hunters, but many investigators have searched the area for the fort's elusive graveyards. Records are incomplete and conflicting, but it is believed that the fort had at least three cemeteries. One of them is thought to be near the parade ground and Officers Row at the U.S. Army's Vancouver Barracks. Another possible site is at the Old City Cemetery, on Mill Plain Boulevard.

By the mid-1840s, American settlement and economic activity in the region pressured British interests into moving farther north. The resulting de facto reorganization of political control of the region was formalized in the Oregon Treaty of 1846, which moved the southern boundary of British territory to the 49th parallel. The treaty enabled local Americans to establish the Oregon Territory, including land that currently comprises the states of Oregon, Washington, and Idaho as well as parts of Wyoming and Montana. After officially recognizing it on August 14, 1848, as an incorporated U.S. territory, Congress authorized the construction of a military facility adjacent to the now-derelict Hudson's Bay fort.

Opened in 1849, the facility was originally known as Camp Vancouver. In the 1850s, various publications referred to it as "Columbia Barracks" and "Fort Vancouver." Ghost hunters who research the history of buildings in the area may be confused by the U.S. Army facility and the earlier Hudson's Bay fort both using the name Fort Vancouver. The army facility and nearby Pearson Field sprawl over land once occupied by parts of the Hudson's Bay settlement, but they are distinct historical entities.

Through the second half of the 19th century, Vancouver Barracks grew to include more than 100 buildings, barns, and shops and several corrals. Among the remaining buildings are several mansions that comprise Officers Row. Each one is distinctive, yet all of them reflect the architectural fashion of the time. Their styles include Second Empire, Italianate, Classical Revival, Queen Anne, and Colonial Revival. The largest mansions were constructed for field officers who held a rank of major or higher. Many of them were once occupied by famous generals, including Ulysses S. Grant, George B. McClellan, and George Pickett. In the 1930s, Gen. George C. Marshall served at the barracks. Throughout World War II, he was U.S. Army chief of staff and chief military adviser to Pres. Franklin D. Roosevelt. After the war, Marshall served as secretary of state under Pres. Harry Truman. He distinguished himself by developing and administering the Marshall Plan, which rebuilt Europe after World War II. His house, believed to be haunted, still stands on Officers Row.

After World War II, military activity at the barracks was minimal. By 1949, most of the fort was transferred to the National Park Service. In 2012, the U.S. Army Reserve vacated all lands and structures within the East and South Vancouver Barracks, marking the end of military activity at the historic site.

Decades of U.S. Army activity, coupled with the dramatic history of early Yankee settlers and the struggles and early demise of Hudson's Bay explorers and fur trappers, have left an indelible paranormal mark on the landscape. Some of the buildings are not currently accessible, but the grounds offer many opportunities for dowsing, EMF and EVP sweeps, and exploration by empaths.

## VANCOUVER BARRACKS HOSPITAL, BUILDING 614

Barnes Street at McClelland Road
Vancouver, WA 98661
360-816-6230
www.nps.gov/places/vbposthospital.htm

Most of the structures that comprise the Post Hospital at Vancouver Barracks were constructed between 1905 and 1907. The oldest portion of the hospital was built in the 1880s and served as an aid station and storage facility for medical supplies that were to be shipped out with troops dispatched to the Indian Wars and Spanish-American War of 1898. During its years of operation, buildings were joined together, porches were enclosed, and, in the 1970s, the southern wing was rotated 90 degrees and attached to the main building to make way for the I-5 widening project. At the height of its development, the hospital had 400 beds, several operating rooms and clinics, a morgue in the basement, and a large psychiatric ward on the third floor. Always busy with sick and injured soldiers, the hospital also served loggers from nearby mills and members of the Civilian Conservation Corps. During the Spanish flu epidemic of 1918, more than 21,000 patients were treated at this hospital. It is unknown how many patients died here, but through the decades during which sick and injured people sought help here, it is likely that thousands left the place by way of the morgue.

The army closed the Post Hospital after World War II but continued to use the building for storage and offices. Early in the 1990s, the last military tenants moved out, and the place has stood vacant since. With the exception of a few fortunate ghost hunters, only maintenance and construction workers have entered the building, trying to stop the ravages of time so that it might someday be repurposed as an inn or offices. Despite their efforts, the building is in rough shape. I was allowed entry during my last visit to Vancouver Barracks. Aside from the basic creepiness of the place, it is dark with paint peeling from the

*The Vancouver Barracks hospital once had 400 beds serving wounded soldiers and thousands stricken with the Spanish flu in 1918.*

walls, cracked and stained ceiling plaster, and some rooms filled with maintenance supplies or piles of dirt and dust. I was told many of the floor tiles contain asbestos.

Most of the credible stories about ghostly activity in this old hospital come from maintenance and construction workers. Doors to the building have been found unlocked when workers arrive in the morning, despite assurances that they were locked by the last person leaving the previous evening. Curious workers have left tape on the doors that would be torn if the doors were opened. When the doors were found unlocked on several occasions and the tape undisturbed, it seemed clear that whoever unlocked the doors did not enter or leave the place.

A ghost hunter visiting from Texas claims she was chased from the basement by an "aggressive" ghost. I encountered an angry spirit in the basement, but there were no gestures that caused me to flee. It was clear, however, that this ghost did not want visitors. His attitude did not change even when I told him that I work in a large hospital. A portion of the basement was used as a morgue, and I found it easy to identify areas where bodies were stored, because the air thickened abruptly and intense cold spots were discovered. One ghost hunter reported seeing an old autopsy table shake. Others have reported what they call "the smell of death" in the basement.

The women's restroom on the second floor has also been identified as a paranormal hotspot. Ghosts in this room raise and lower the toilet-seat lids. At several places throughout the hospital, workers have heard unexplained footsteps, keys jingling as if a ghost night watchman were walking about, coughing, moaning, loud bangs that echo down hallways, tapping sounds emanating from the walls, muted whispers, and creaking noises as if doors were opening on old, rusty hinges.

Today, the Fort Vancouver National Trust hopes to partner with other civic organizations and fully renovate the Post Hospital into a center for the arts. Glass-enclosed porches that once housed tuberculosis patients may be repurposed as artist studios, and large rooms that were once busy wards may be suitable for performance arts or meetings. When the place does reopen to the public, ghost hunters should be among the first visitors to learn what the ghosts think of the renovation and modern amenities.

## HOWARD HOUSE

750 Anderson Street
Vancouver, WA 98661
360-992-1800
www.thehistorictrust.org/tours1/o-o-howard-house

Strange things have happened in this house, causing many people to conclude that it is haunted. No one has identified the ghosts that occupy the mansion, but it is clear that at least one spirit has the power to break glass.

The house was constructed in 1879 as a residence for Maj. Gen. Oliver Otis Howard (1830-1909) and his family. A Medal of Honor winner, General Howard fought in several major battles of the Civil War, including Gettysburg, and lost his right arm in 1862 after suffering two gunshot wounds at the Battle of Fair Oaks. After the war, he played a major role in Reconstruction. In 1874 he assumed command of the Department of the Columbia and established his headquarters at Fort Vancouver. Over the next six years, he fought in several Indian wars, which nearly wiped out formerly peaceful tribes of the Pacific Northwest, including the Nez Perce led by Chief Joseph. Dubbed the "Christian General" because of his religious beliefs, Howard was known for considering spiritual issues in the development of his military policies, including battle plans. For several days after his return to Fort Vancouver from a battle, he was often seen pacing the mansion's wide porch or walking past the large windows on the second floor. This suggests he was deeply affected by the destruction of a culture that, at times, he defended against bureaucrats in Washington, D.C. Perhaps it is his ghost that witnesses have spotted passing by the large windows on the second floor.

The most reliable report of this ghostly manifestation is that of a former fort commander who walked past the Howard mansion one night with his son. At the time, the house was awaiting renovation after a fire, and much of it was boarded up. Both witnesses saw a white, humanoid figure pass by several second-floor windows. It moved from one end of the house to the other numerous times over a five-minute period.

Ghostly activity seems to have occurred on the first floor of the mansion as well. One morning in 1999, workers entered to find that an exhibit composed of 20 large glass panels had been vandalized. One panel, measuring four by eight feet, lay in pieces on the floor. The initial suggestion that a ghost was responsible was dismissed as a joke. However, a few years later a similar event occurred. During a recent visit of mine, a person who works in the house told me that strange things happen "all the time." Usually, these are doors that swing open and closed, muffled footsteps, and unexplained cold spots. Once,

*The ghost of Civil War hero Maj. Gen. Oliver Howard still paces the second-floor rooms of his former home.*

a security system that tracked movements captured someone moving from a second-floor room to the hallway and into another room before disappearing from surveillance.

General Howard resided in this beautiful mansion only two years before his appointment as superintendent of the United States Military Academy at West Point. Upon his retirement from the army on November 8, 1894, at the age of 64, he established his residence at his daughter's home in Portland, where he wrote his memoirs. Today, the Howard House is headquarters of the Fort Vancouver National Trust. Rooms may be rented for meetings and small receptions and the courtyard for weddings.

## ARTILLERY BARRACKS

Fort Vancouver
600 East Hatheway Road
Vancouver, WA 98661
360-828-5237
www.historictrustproperties.org/property/artillery-barracks

Constructed in 1904, the artillery barracks were designed to house a battalion of up to 240 men. A Spartan military facility, the 40,000-square-foot building had a few architectural flourishes, such as a pressed-tin ceiling and fancy white-oak floors. These features were restored to their original glory when the entire building was renovated and reopened as a conference center. Today, meeting and banquet rooms can be rented by the hour.

Despite the modern conveniences, the place still has a military atmosphere, which includes a few ghosts. No one knows how many soldiers may have died in the building, but it seems certain that some would have perished here during the Spanish flu epidemic of 1918. When members of a battalion came down with flu or other contagious illnesses, the men were usually quarantined in their barracks. During my visits to the building, I encountered shuffling footsteps, as though sick men were struggling to walk from their beds to the latrine. These odd footfalls were often accompanied by muted coughs. This building is large enough that a ghost hunter may get away from others and conduct EVP sweeps or use dowsing rods without attracting unwanted attention. A hotspot for paranormal activity is the center of the large conference room. In 1904, this area was the sergeant's walk, a path that noncommissioned officers walked while monitoring the troops whose bunks filled the space between the outer walls and the columns that still stand.

## GHOST ON THE STAIRS

George C. Marshall House
1301 Officers Row
Vancouver, WA 98661

360-693-3103
www.historictrustproperties.org/property/marshall-house

Built in 1886 as a residence for the barracks commander and his family, this spectacular mansion has been occupied by so many people that it is impossible to determine whose ghost haunts the place. EVP and psychic investigations have not led to an identification of the ghost, but I believe that it is the spirit of a maid who worked in the house for many years.

The mansion is named in honor of Gen. George C. Marshall (1880-1959), although he resided in the house with his wife, Katharine, for only a few years, from 1936 to 1938. Marshall is well known to history buffs as the U.S. Army chief of staff throughout World War II and secretary of state from 1947 to 1949. His greatest postwar accomplishment was the Marshall Plan, which rebuilt Europe and many of the Pacific nations. For this great service to humanity, he was awarded the Nobel Peace Prize. During his three years at Vancouver Barracks, he commanded the Third Division's Fifth Infantry Brigade and organized the region's Civilian Conservation Corps camps.

The interior of the Queen Anne-style Victorian mansion is nothing short of spectacular. Elegant mirrors and fireplace surrounds, distinctive inlaid hardwood floors, period furniture, and amazing wood paneling create a fascinating 19th-century atmosphere. I found the general's study on the first floor and the staircase to be the most active sites for paranormal activity.

For nearly 30 minutes, I sat on the small bench on the staircase landing between the first and second floors, detecting the presence of a female ghost who walked up and down the stairs while humming. At times, I also heard a distinct grunt, as though she had lost her breath while carrying something heavy. I believe that this ghost was a maid in the house who is eternally bound to continue her duties, cleaning the place and carrying heavy loads of laundry from the second-floor bedrooms to the basement.

In the general's study, I detected the presence of a very old gentleman who sits quietly at the desk, watching people who tour the house. He does not seem to object to strangers in the study, but he is quite curious about why they are there and not wearing military uniforms.

Today, this Victorian mansion is a museum open for tours, providing easy access for ghost hunters. Rooms are available for rent for special events and, on the second floor, as office space.

## GHOST OF GENERAL SULLY

Grant House
1101 Officers Row
Vancouver, WA 98661
360-816-6230
www.nps.gov/articles/granthouse.htm

Although Gen. Ulysses S. Grant never lived in this house, it bears his name in recognition of his service at Fort Vancouver from 1852 to 1853. He resided in the Quartermaster's Ranch while at the fort, but it is likely he spent a lot of time in this building. Constructed in 1848 as a log building, the place was used briefly as the fort commander's residence before renovation as the officers' club. With the addition of wide verandas surrounding the first and second floors and wood panels over the logs, the house's architecture became reminiscent of a mid-Atlantic mansion, which was probably quite appealing to the many officers who were thousands of miles from their homes in Virginia and the Carolinas. During the Civil War, the building returned to use as a residence for commanding officers, one of whom was Gen. Alfred Sully (1821-79), who gained fame in the Indian Wars of the 1860s.

General Sully arrived in Monterey, California, in 1849, enthused by his assignment to such idyllic country. Soon after his arrival, at the age of 28, he married a 15-year-old Mexican girl and contemplated leaving the army for the life of a farmer and rancher in this pristine land. Tragedy struck, however, when his young wife succumbed to cholera and his child died of strangulation. Deeply embittered by their loss, he thrust himself into his military career, which culminated in his appointment as commander of Fort Vancouver from 1874 to 1879.

In his book, *No Tears for the General: The Life of General Alfred Sully 1821-1879*, Sully's grandson, Langdon Sully, noted that the general never recovered from the loss of his young family. Other biographers suggest that this personal anguish accounts for Sully's reputation as "a hard-bitten, unemotional soldier." It also explains why the general's ghost haunts the Grant House, a place where he may have found solace from the misery of losing his wife and baby.

Later in life, Sully was described in newspaper accounts as a somber and stoic fellow. In 1877, the *Vancouver Independent* described his appearance as he reviewed troops: "The General looks venerable with his silver locks, and gives the command

*Constructed as a log building in 1848, the Grant House is haunted by one of its most illustrious residents, Gen. Alfred Sully.*

with a stern dignity born of a long experience in Army life." Ghost hunters who search the Grant House for General Sully should be on the lookout for a man of stern demeanor with long, gray-silver hair.

Ghostly activity attributed to Sully includes cold spots, footsteps on wood floors, doors opening and closing, windows rattling, telephones and other electrical devices turning on, and disembodied voices whispering in the ears of surprised visitors. Sully also seems to like coffee. Staff have found coffeemakers turned on when they arrive in the morning. Sometimes, they discover a half-cup of coffee on a table and a chair pulled away.

Local author Jeff Davis has visited the Grant House often and believes that the general was sick for a long time before he died. "I think he may have had stomach cancer," Davis noted. "Others think it was kidney problems. Sometimes he couldn't get out of bed and other times he'd pace the hall all night because of the pain." It is worth noting that General Sully died in this house on April 27, 1879.

One of the owners of the restaurant that formerly occupied the Grant House has reported seeing a black apparition in a hall on the second floor. Others have spotted a tall man standing on the balcony. This fellow reportedly had a beard and wore an old-fashioned long coat that resembled a military coat.

I have spotted an apparition each time I visit the Grant House. Hotspots include the second-floor hallway outside the room where Sully died, the west balcony, the bar and fireplace, and the first-floor corridor where the building's original log structure is exposed.

EVP investigations may be more productive if you use the general's personal information to elicit a response. You might mention the loss of his young wife in Monterey or ask about his service in the Indian Wars. It has been reported that, in 1862, the general married a French-Yankton Sioux girl because she resembled his late wife. Questions about his Native American wife may evoke responses that suggest this is a sensitive issue.

## GHOST OF THELMA TAYLOR

Cathedral Park
6636 North Baltimore Avenue
Portland 97203
503-823-7529
www.portland.gov/parks/cathedral-park

Thelma Taylor died near the St. Johns Bridge in the 1940s, but her tragic story continues to fascinate people in the neighborhood. Some of them are quite advanced in age, yet they clearly remember Thelma as a quiet, shy girl who worked hard in school and availed herself of every opportunity to make a little money by picking beans or cleaning houses. Their recollections in recent interviews have introduced Thelma to a new generation of people who are fascinated by tragic crimes and the ghosts they produce.

Fifteen-year-old Thelma was murdered on August 6, 1949, by 22-year-old Morris Leland after a miserable night huddled in the tall reeds and shrubs that covered the ground near the St. Johns Bridge. Thelma was kidnapped early in the morning on August 5. Leland admitted that he initially tried to befriend Thelma and, despite her misgivings, she made no attempt to escape. After driving around for an hour, Leland parked the car and kept Thelma in a secluded area near the Willamette River for the remainder of the day. Intending to rape her, he deferred when he learned she was a virgin. Throughout the day, long periods of silence were interrupted by brief conversation. Eventually, Leland grew tired of Thelma and the dangerous predicament he had created. With a long criminal record that began when he was only 13 years old, he knew that one more encounter with the Portland police would end with a significant prison sentence. Previous arrests for assault, rape, car theft, and robbery should have deterred him, but the prospect of more jail time had not been sufficient to stop him from committing one more heinous crime. Perhaps his beguiling demeanor and the seven-inch hunting knife he carried gave him the confidence to follow his baser instincts.

Sometime in the evening, Leland realized he could not release Thelma because she was a responsible girl who would promptly report the incident to the police. It was also clear that she would be able to give police a good description of the car and Leland himself. Concerned about being seen, he moved Thelma to another vacant lot about eight blocks north of the St. Johns Bridge.

After hours of pleading and crying, Thelma fell asleep as Leland sat brooding about the inevitable murder of a girl he wished he had never encountered. He fell asleep just before dawn, while Thelma awakened to the sound of railroads cars moving along a nearby track. Sensing an opportunity for help, Thelma started screaming. Leland, startled, grabbed a piece of steel rebar that had been discarded in the junk-strewn lot. After the first blow to her head, Thelma stopped screaming, yet Leland continued beating her. When it was clear she was dead, he plunged his knife deep into her abdomen.

Leland hid Thelma's body under logs and brush then escaped, only to be apprehended a week later while driving a stolen car. Police were aware of a missing person's report concerning Thelma Taylor but did not look upon Leland as a suspect. Plagued by guilt or simply tired of his miserable life, Leland asked to speak to a homicide detective about a murder he had committed. On February 7, 1951, Morris Leland was convicted of first-degree murder and sentenced to death. That sentence was carried out on January 9, 1953, in the gas chamber at the state penitentiary in Salem.

All of that horror and misery happened so long ago, yet something paranormal persists in the places where Leland held Thelma captive before murdering her. The ground under the St. Johns Bridge is now known as Cathedral Park, by virtue of the gothic design of the bridge's supporting structure. It opened as a beautiful park in the 1980s, and the tall reeds and weeds that once concealed Thelma from the help of passersby are now gone. Her ghost may still be there, however, screaming in the predawn air.

The proprietor of a nearby café has heard a young girl's voice cry out, "Help me! Help me! Somebody, please!" Others in the neighborhood told me they have heard two voices, a male and a female, arguing in the middle of the night.

People who live near Cathedral Park also report strange lights moving around in the darkness and unexplained cold spots. Sensitives feel dread and anguish in the stand of trees that fills a depression slightly northwest of the bridge. This is likely the spot where Thelma spent the last night of her life.

These sounds and impressions may be imprints left behind from that harrowing night on August 5, 1949, because it seems unlikely to me that Thelma would remain in a place where

*Locals believe that the ghost of Thelma Taylor still haunts Cathedral Park, the site of a terrifying kidnapping and tragic murder.*

she was held captive at knifepoint and sexually abused. It is possible, however, that her ghost remains in Cathedral Park, unaware that she is dead or unable to accept the notion that she is free to leave.

It is important to note that Thelma was not killed in Cathedral Park. Based on Leland's confession, her body was found a few blocks north of the park close to the Willamette River. I explored that location by walking north on North Bradford Street until I reached the eastern boundary of a large container yard. As I headed to the shore of the river, my dowsing rods became extremely active. At one spot about 15 feet from the water, near a pile of logs similar to those that once concealed Thelma's body, the rods began spinning and continued to do so for more than two minutes. They stopped when I asked, "Thelma, are you here?"

## HISTORIC COLUMBIAN CEMETERY

1151 North Columbia Boulevard
Portland 97211
609-628-2297
www.steelmantowncemetery.com/historic_columbian_cemetery.html

Creepy yet beautiful, this old cemetery contains the remains of some of Portland's earliest pioneers. Among them are key players in the city's evolution from a muddy, backwater logging town to a major Pacific Rim port. Despite the efforts of dedicated volunteers who provide 100 percent of the funds necessary for the cemetery's maintenance, many headstones have suffered from vandalism and neglect. Others are simply worn by the climate, making the inscriptions almost illegible. Opened in 1857 at the shore of the Columbia Slough, the tiny cemetery is now surrounded by freeway ramps that convey traffic to and from I-5. A dense tree canopy provides a barrier to the sound of cars and trucks and creates still air and shadows that enable sensitive visitors to get in touch with the spirits of

Portland's pioneers who await help clearing or repairing graves. Many visitors have reported experiences with a ghost of Lydia, who seems to have assumed the duty of cemetery hostess. She whispers in the ears of fascinated visitors and sometimes appears as a partial apparition. I could not find a headstone engraved with *Lydia,* but many monuments in this cemetery were obscured by piles of leaves and tall grass. As I walked the alleys between rows of graves, I did encounter cells of thickened air that were much cooler than the surrounding atmosphere.

The graves of Andreas Schmidt (1827-1910) and his wife, Amelia (1830-1908), are particularly fascinating because they are surrounded by the graves of their children and grandchildren. The graves of the Adams family are just as

*Opened in 1857, beautifully creepy Columbian Cemetery contains the remains of some of Portland's earliest pioneers.*

compelling and thought-provoking. Little Frankie (1876) lived less than a year, while Sethie (1873-79) lived to age six. Patriarch Asa Adams (1804-77) lived a long life but had to endure the passing of his wife, Hannah (1816-73), and grandson Frankie. Strong imprints may be found here, undoubtedly created by Adams family members who visited the graves on birthdays and other important dates.

As I walked around the cemetery, I perceived several strange sounds. Being completely alone and blocking out the noise of nearby traffic, I heard the muted tones of musical instruments, horse's hooves on the muddy ground, and a gunshot that echoed off the wall of a warehouse that stands adjacent to the east border of the cemetery.

CHAPTER 5

# Communities South of Portland

Oregon City, Salem, Eugene, and other communities linked by I-5 are often visited by travelers heading to or away from Portland. This modern highway makes transit easy, leaving you time and energy to stop and spend an hour or two touring the many historical sites. Ghost hunters who take the opportunity to look into the histories of these communities will find fascinating tales of pioneer families who traveled for months on the arduous Oregon Trail, arriving a decade or more before Oregon became the 33rd U.S. state on February 14, 1859. The homes they built, the towns they founded, and the cemeteries they filled remain as intriguing sites for those who wish to experience the ghosts of some of Oregon's great families. Modern tragedies have created a fresh crop of ghosts, but it is particularly fascinating to seek out spirits from some of Oregon's pioneers, such as Dr. Forbes Barclay, Dr. John McLoughlin, Asahel and Eugenia Bush, Gen. Cyrus Reed, the McMurphey daughters, and little Josephine Hunsaker, who died at the tender age of 12. Visit the Ermatinger house, where Francis Pettygrove and Asa Lovejoy flipped the coin that decided if the booming, muddy city to the north should be called Boston or Portland. Enjoy the scenery and ease of travel on I-5, but do take the time to visit with Oregon's historical ghosts.

## GHOST OF THE FATHER OF OREGON

McLoughlin House
713 Center Street

Oregon City 97045
503-656-5146
www.mcloughlinhouse.org

The McLoughlin House stands today as an iconic structure that calls to mind Oregon's greatest pioneer, Dr. John McLoughlin (1784-1857), and his effect on the history of Fort Vancouver, Oregon City, and Oregon. Originally constructed in 1845 on a steep hillside by the Willamette River, the grand two-story house was slated for demolition in 1909 until concerned citizens stepped forward. They founded the McLoughlin Memorial Association and quickly mustered the resources to move the house to its current location on a bluff subsequently named McLoughlin Ridge. After a lengthy restoration process, the place opened as a museum that contains many pieces of furniture used by the McLoughlin family.

Despite its distinction as the grandest home in Oregon City, the McLoughlin House has a dark past. Ten years after the doctor's death in 1857, his daughter, Marie Eloisa McLoughlin Harvey (1817-84), sold the mansion, and it reopened as a hotel. Its location near the rapidly growing industrial part of town fostered its transition into a dormitory for workers at a nearby woolen mill and then into a brothel. Ultimately, it was abandoned to vagrants, who nearly destroyed the place. The McLoughlin Memorial Association saved it only weeks before its planned demolition. Today, the McLoughlin House is the oldest museum in Oregon. It is notable that McLoughlin and his wife, Marguerite (1775-1860), both died in the home. Their graves, located in the backyard, were moved from the original site.

Born in Quebec in 1784, McLoughlin was a quintessential pioneer who literally created a new civilization in a land thousands of miles from his home. From the age of six, he lived with his great-uncle, who generously supported the boy's education. McLoughlin received a medical degree at a very young age in 1803. As a physician working for the Northwest Company, a fur-trading enterprise, he traveled extensively throughout Canada and mastered several Indian languages.

In 1824, Hudson's Bay Company hired him as chief factor (superintendent) of the Columbia District. Arriving in Oregon country in 1825, he established Fort Vancouver, where he regulated trade in the region, kept peace with the Indians, and developed salmon fisheries and the timber industry as well as export businesses that sent goods as far as Russian Alaska, Mexican California, and Hawaii. He also maintained amicable relations between American and British fur trappers, whose numbers increased rapidly throughout the 1830s. By the 1840s, friction between British and American interests in the region had escalated, and McLoughlin found himself favoring Yankee immigration and settlement, despite orders from his superiors to discourage such encroachment. In 1842, he supported the formation of Oregon as an independent nation, but this notion was dropped when American settlers called for a provisional government that would ultimately create Oregon Territory as part of the United States. McLoughlin favored that movement, and in 1846, representatives of the British Crown joined American representatives in signing the Oregon Treaty.

McLoughlin immediately resigned from the British-owned Hudson's Bay Company and founded a town about 30 miles south of the Columbia River on the banks of the Willamette. Possibly as a demonstration of his true allegiance, he named the town Oregon City.

In many accounts of Oregon's history, McLoughlin is described as an able administrator, skilled and caring physician, shrewd politician, wise diplomat, visionary, and congenial host to both white settlers and local Indians. He stood six feet five inches tall and, in his later years, wore long white hair and a stern countenance. Local Indians, who revered him for his fairness, called him the "Silver-Haired Eagle." His marriage to Marguerite, a half-Cree, half-Swiss woman, not only reflected his attitude toward Native Americans but enhanced his popularity with them.

This old house is reportedly full of spirits. In addition to the spirits of McLoughlin and his wife, ghosts may be found here that were "created" when the place was a hotel, brothel, and vagrants' flophouse.

*Once the home of Dr. John McLoughlin, known as the Father of Oregon, this 1845-vintage house is now a museum that harbors several ghosts.*

McLoughlin's presence has been detected at several locations within the mansion. Visitors and museum staff members have heard unexplained footsteps on the stairs, in the parlor, and in an upstairs bedroom. A tall shadow believed to be the doctor has been spotted on the stairs, in the parlor, and in the dining room. A portrait of McLoughlin hangs over the fireplace in the parlor, where he died. It is said that every year on September 3, the anniversary of his death, the doctor's painted face glows eerily.

An apparition, unmistakably identified as McLoughlin, has been seen sitting on the bed in the master bedroom. This ghost often sits in a rocking chair, making it rock back and forth.

Passersby on the street have reported seeing the image of a woman, identified as Marguerite McLoughlin, looking out an upstairs window. Marguerite was known for smoking a pipe, and several people have detected the peculiar odor of pipe tobacco in an upstairs bedroom. She has also been known to hover close to or touch visitors and staff members and move out-of-reach objects such as her china tea set.

In the 1880s, Chinese workers at the nearby woolen mills were housed in the building. There is no historical record of deaths, but it seems likely that several of them died there, because psychics have detected a number of spirits in the office who are frightened of something. They create an aura in the room that some psychics sense as quite disturbing or negative.

Some writers have reported that a murder occurred in the parlor, probably during the time that the place was a brothel or vagrants' camp. Sensitive people who enter the room experience an abrupt and intense impression of foreboding. Some break into a sweat and feel they must get out of the house immediately.

The most frequently sighted ghost in the McLoughlin House has been dubbed the "red-haired boy." Judged to be six to eight years old, he appears as a lifelike apparition at several locations there and in the nearby Barclay House. He has been spotted playing near the stairs, in the dining rooms, and in the offices of these homes. Often, the boy is accompanied by the partial apparition of a dog, which leaves muddy footprints. This child has been so active in the houses that, at times, the police have been called to investigate an intruder. His antics include hiding objects needed by staff members and watching visitors as they tour the houses. It seems likely that the red-haired boy was a child of Eloisa McLoughlin. However, I was unable to locate any historical records that describe the hair color of her three boys.

Sensitive people who tour the house detect fascinating and sometimes unpleasant sensations. A group of Native Americans once entered but stopped abruptly when they encountered something that they described as "unpleasant." It is difficult to imagine what may have created that impression, because McLoughlin was known for his kindness toward local Indians and he was highly respected by them. One psychic reported that she detected the presence of a protective Indian who was once a servant in the McLoughlin House. The spirit of the servant may still be on duty, safeguarding his fortunate position within the household.

## GHOST OF UNCLE SANDY

Barclay House
719 Center Street
Oregon City 97045
www.mcloughlinhouse.org/the-barclay-house.html

Built in 1849 as a residence for Dr. Forbes Barclay and his family, this house now stands next to the McLoughlin House, part of a cluster of historic homes once occupied by Oregon City's greatest pioneers. The house stood at the Oregon City waterfront until the 1930s, when it was moved to its current site on McLoughlin Ridge. It no longer commands a view of the Willamette River, but shaded by tall trees, it is still a popular venue for ghost hunters.

In his early life, Dr. Forbes Barclay (1812-73) was somewhat of an adventurer. He embarked on several Arctic expeditions, including one that ended in a shipwreck from which he was saved by Inuit. Deciding to settle down, he took his medical degree from the Royal College of Surgeons in 1838 and entered into service with the Hudson's Bay Company, based in eastern Canada. Still longing for adventure, Dr. Barclay headed west to Fort Vancouver, arriving June 4, 1839. There he met Dr. John McLoughlin, the famed superintendent of the fort who, years later, enticed Barclay to move to Oregon City.

While at Fort Vancouver, Barclay married Marie Pambrun (1826-90), who was not yet 16 years old. The eldest daughter of Chief Trader Pierre Chrysologue Pambrun and Catherine Humpherville, the French-speaking beauty was widely known for her fine character and trace of Indian blood. She and Barclay had seven children together. Their first child, Jean Jacques, died of diphtheria in 1847, at age two. Their two other boys, Peter Thomas (1847-unknown) and Alexander (1849-1908), moved with the Barclays into their new Oregon City house in 1849. The couple had four more children, all of whom were born in the Barclay House: Adrianna "Katie" Catherine (1852-1934), Hattie (1854-1926), William Charles (1856-1926), and Edmund (1859-63).

Numerous relatives visited the house often, some staying for several months. It has been reported that Barclay's seafaring brother, "Uncle Sandy," stayed there whenever his ship docked in Portland and that his spirit now haunts the place. I wonder if this is an error perpetuated by the retelling of a popular ghost story. I could find no record of Barclay's nine siblings, aside from James, who was a teacher at Larwick, in the Shetland Islands. Barclay's son William Charles was an accomplished sailor, however. Beginning his career on windjammers, he sailed the world, experiencing eight shipwrecks and accumulating a large collection of guns he confiscated from Chinese pirates. He retired from the transport service of the United States Navy with the rank of captain and died on March 10, 1926, at the Marine Hospital in San Francisco. I wonder if he is the ghost that has been spotted sitting in a chair at the Barclay House, glaring at people who enter his room.

William may have been "Uncle Sandy" to Hattie's children, who resided elsewhere in town but were constantly in the house visiting their aunt Katie. Though childless, Katie had taken over the house as her residence after her father's death.

Ghost hunters may resolve this issue of identity by performing an EVP sweep in which questions are posed regarding childhood, encounters with Chinese pirates, and rank achieved. If audio recordings capture a disembodied voice that claims to be a captain born in Oregon (while denying a childhood in Scotland), we might conclude that "Uncle Sandy" is Barclay's son.

The ghost of a red-haired little boy has been spotted in the Barclay House, too. Estimated to be six to eight years old, he is playful. He hides tools and other small objects and often plays near the front door. He shows up next door in the McLoughlin House as well.

The Barclay House was used by family descendants until 1934, when it was deeded to the city and moved from its original location at the waterfront. It is now used as a gift shop, featuring unique books about Pacific Northwest history, and as a National Park Service visitor's center. Psychics claim to have encountered the spirits of Barclay and his wife here, who seem to be unaware of visitors and changes that have occurred inside the home. The couple died in the house, as did their daughters, Hattie and Katie.

## ERMATINGER HOUSE

Sixth Street at John Adams Street
Oregon City 97045
www.orcity.org/parksandrecreation/ermatinger-house

At least one ghost haunts this fascinating home, but the Ermatinger House's historical significance is due to a momentous event that took place in its parlor in 1845. During a dinner party hosted by Francis and Catherine Ermatinger, Francis Pettygrove and Asa Lovejoy began a spirited discussion about land they owned downriver at a spot often referred to as "the clearing." Lovejoy argued that it should be called Boston, after his hometown, while Pettygrove insisted that a better name was Portland, like his own hometown in Maine. A coin, tossed into the air three times by Ermatinger, settled the issue. Pettygrove won two out of three tosses, and today, the city in "the clearing" is called Portland.

The Ermatinger House is one of the oldest in the state of Oregon and is distinguished as the only two-story Federal-style home originally built with a flat roof sheathed with tin. Born in Portugal, Francis Ermatinger (1798-1858) obtained an education in England before immigrating to Canada, where he found employment with the Hudson's Bay Company in 1818. In 1825, he transferred to Fort Vancouver and worked for Dr. John McLoughlin. He met and married McLoughlin's granddaughter, Catherine Sinclair, and secured a transfer to an outpost on the Willamette River that would later be named Oregon City. In 1844, McLoughlin deeded to Ermatinger the land on which this house was built in 1845. Francis and Catherine lived there only a short time before he was transferred to another Hudson's Bay enterprise. In 1849, the house was sold and for the next 60 years it was occupied by various families. It was moved from its riverfront location to

*The Ermatinger House was the scene of a famous coin toss in 1845 that granted the winner, Francis Pettygrove, the right to name a muddy village downriver "Portland."*

Center Street in 1910. Years later, it was moved again, to its current site in the McLoughlin Historical District. Historical records do not help us determine who may be haunting the house, but it is clear that something paranormal is attached to the place.

The last time I toured the home, it was undergoing extensive renovation that had attracted the attention of at least one ghost. I detected a spirit who seemed angered that a fireplace was missing. Historical records show that two fireplaces once existed on the first floor, but they were removed to facilitate the move from the riverfront location. The fellow I encountered seemed quite agitated about the changes.

## STEVENS-CRAWFORD HERITAGE HOUSE

603 Sixth Street
Oregon City 97045

(503) 655-2866
www.clackamashistory.org/schh

Constructed in 1908 by Oregon pioneer Harley Stevens and his wife, Elizabeth Stevens Crawford, this fascinating American Foursquare-style house is now a museum. Stevens (1847-1924) arrived in Oregon in 1862 at the age of 15 and worked for the railroad as a telegraph operator and depot agent. In 1871, he married Mary Elizabeth Crawford (1850-1932), with whom he had two children, Harley Jr. and Muriel "Mertie" (1872-1968). At the age of 36, Mertie moved with the family into the new house and resided there until her death. Diagnosed as a "sickly child," she was advised not to marry or attempt to have children. Thus she lived a spinster's life, but she enjoyed great popularity in Oregon City. Appreciating the historical value of the home's furnishings and other artifacts, Mertie bequeathed the entire property to the Clackamas County Historical Society upon her death. The house, including the Stevens family's cherished possessions, is now open to the public.

Is this charming old home haunted? Many ghost hunters in the area believe that spirits wander through the parlor, dining room, and quaint kitchen. Northwest Ghost Tours includes this grand old house in its popular two-hour tour. Numerous artifacts most certainly contain imprints of Mertie and others who spent time in the home. The ghost of Harley Stevens may occupy the house, looking after family heirlooms, including pictures of his little girl, Mertie.

When I toured the home and grounds, I felt strangely familiar with the place. The house is similar to many in my hometown, Alameda, California. Beyond that, I sensed that the spirits who remained in the house were quite at ease. None of them felt threatened or bothered by modern persons who staffed the place or tourists who wandered from room to room, expressing curiosity about the way people lived in the early 20th century.

## JOSEPHINE'S ROSE

Mountain View Cemetery
500 Hilda Street

Oregon City 97045
503-657-8299
www.orcity.org/cemetery

Mountain View Cemetery encapsulates the quintessential Oregon landscape, with rolling green fields, a running creek, and tall trees standing against a brilliant sky. The monuments placed here by loving family members to commemorate the lives of deceased spouses, parents, or children, however, remind us that life is precious and often cut short by unforeseen tragedy. Aside from durable granite headstones with fascinating epitaphs, other offerings, far more ethereal, may arouse a visitor's emotions. These mark a spot where century-old imprints may produce a paranormal experience.

The most fascinating of these fragile offerings is Josephine's rosebush, which has flourished at the grave of a young girl since the 19th century. After an arduous journey on the famed Oregon Trail, Josephine Hunsaker's family arrived in Oregon City in 1846. The bountiful land enabled them to flourish and help others newly arrived in town and desperate for aid. In the winter of 1853, however, the Hunsaker family found itself in need of help, as 12-year-old Josephine became ill with diphtheria or typhoid fever. Throughout February, she lay in her bed, gazing out the window at green hills and, perhaps, spotting other children at play. Dr. John McLoughlin visited often and, one day, realized that Josephine should have something special to gaze upon. He pulled a rosebush from his garden, potted it, and placed it outside her window. It was winter and the plant was not in bloom, but the good doctor probably hoped that its graceful little branches and few remaining leaves might give Josephine hope that she and the rosebush would flourish in the spring. Sadly, she died on March 10, 1853. This tragedy was soon followed by the death of Josephine's 11 year old brother, Horton.

After burying her two children side by side so that they could be together for eternity, Mrs. Hunsaker realized that Josephine might be comforted by having her rosebush at her grave. Thus, it was transplanted and nurtured for many years until Mrs. Hunsaker passed away. The rosebush remains there to this day, despite considerable damage inflicted by groundskeepers who were unaware of its significance. Now protected by a fence, it stands as if something exceptional or paranormal has kept it alive. Psychics who visit the grave sense an energy there that may be an imprint created by Mrs. Hunsaker, who doubtless visited it often, or Josephine, lending her spiritual vigor to the beloved rosebush.

The children's gravesite is on the left as you enter the grounds (in the pioneer section of the cemetery), surrounded by a black fence.

Another fascinating site within this graveyard is the McCune family tomb. Also located in the pioneer section at the north side of the cemetery, this tomb is larger than nearby monuments and is crumbling apart. Several bricks seem to be missing, and the mortar is decayed. As I approached, I sensed a wall of energy, as if a spirit was quite disturbed by the current state of this tomb. Typically, whenever headstones or other monuments are damaged by storms or fallen trees, ghosts are aroused and may stand at the tomb, awaiting the help of anyone who might replace the bricks.

Many graves in this cemetery will capture the imaginations of ghost hunters who also love history. The first grave to be placed here was that of John Barclay, who died at the age of two in 1847 while residing at Fort Vancouver. Another old grave is that of Dr. William Allen, who died June 9, 1851. Graves with the most intense paranormal activity seem to be those of children.

## MASS MURDER HOUSE

2580 Fisher Road NE
Salem 97305

While staring at the vacant lot at the corner of Beverly Avenue NE and Fisher Road NE, sensitive ghost hunters may become overwhelmed by the energy that lingers here. A house once stood at this place, and it seemed to be a happy home for Nikolay and Natalya Lazukin and their three daughters. The tiny house, tucked into a modest but well-kept neighborhood, may have been occupied by something other than a happy family, however. At 6:03 on the morning of May 22, 2012, Nikolay Lazukin sent a text to his father-in-law that read, “Please forgive me. They took control of my body and did it. I begged them not to but they did. I’m so sorry. Please God forgive me. My last fight I have lost at Exit 174.”

This bizarre message suggests Nikolay had been battling demons or some other malevolent force for some time. During the night, this powerful force overwhelmed him and he committed mass murder. Natalya died from two gunshots to her head. Three-year-old Angelica also died of two gunshots to the head, while Zoe, almost two, was shot once. Baby Sulamia, four month olds, died of traumatic asphyxiation. Before leaving the house, Nikolay dowsed the place with a flammable liquid and set it ablaze. Firefighters arrived at 5:28 A.M. as the neighborhood awoke to a horrible tragedy.

Later that morning, Nikolay was found at Exit 174 slumped in the backseat of his Jeep Cherokee, dead from a self-inflicted gunshot wound to the head. Toxicology reports ruled out a drug, alcohol, or neurological basis for his murderous behavior.

This tragedy may not have been limited to the Lazukin family. Investigators suspect that Nikolay may have killed 21-year-old Devin Matlock, whose body was found near Fisher Road only a few hours after the fire was extinguished.

By all accounts, Nikolay loved his family, yet it seems clear that some powerful, malevolent force gained control of his mind, causing him to murder his wife and children. As I stood at the periphery of the vacant lot where the Lazukin house once stood, I felt that I should not enter the space. I was unable to discover any indication of a burial ground or other spiritual significance of the lot linked to Native Americans. Something must be there, underground or in another dimension, however. The remains of the Lazukin house have been completely removed except for a portion of the driveway. No one has taken a chance and built a new structure at this site.

If you visit this vacant lot, take steps to protect yourself against any malevolent spirits who still reside there. Wear a St. Benedict’s medal and a Christian cross, carry a packet of protective herbs and minerals, and cross your forehead with holy water. Do not actually enter the lot.

## COMMUNITY OF MISERY

Fairview Hospital and Training Center
2250 Strong Road SE
Salem 97302
503-986-5050

The creepiest place in Oregon may be the Fairview Training Center in Salem. Unfortunately for ghost hunters, it may also be the most inaccessible place, since the grounds are closed to visitors, and ominous signs warn those who consider trespassing that they may face a speedy prosecution. It is possible, however, to get a good look at it and even feel some of the negative energy that remains there by approaching the broken fences or the single strands of chain that are intended to keep visitors out. Infrared imaging, either video or still, may capture the many spirits that roam this place at night. The history of this hospital and fascinating reports of paranormal activity posted by reliable investigators attract those who want to have an intense ghostly encounter.

Construction of this large collection of buildings, tunnels, wells, and farm facilities began in 1907, when Oregon created the State Institution for the Feeble-Minded. Late in 1908, the first 39 residents were transferred from the Oregon State Insane Asylum. The center had 670 acres for gardens, orchards, a dairy, and small farm animals, which provided stabilizing and instructional activity for inmates while enabling the institute to be nearly self-sufficient in food production. By 1911, the inmate population was 181, with 25 awaiting admission.

In 1917, the state's commitment law was changed, and Fairview was no longer permitted to admit people who were legally declared insane. Inmates were described as "feeble-minded," but the community also included those with epilepsy and mental retardation. Elimination of an age minimum in

1921, allowing admission of infants, caused the population to rise from 389 to about 950 by 1928. In addition, admission was now open to orphans, hitchhikers, promiscuous girls, those with Down syndrome, and drug abusers. Community sensitivities later changed, and in 1933, the facility became known as the Oregon Fairview Home. Throughout World War II, its population continued to soar, reaching a peak number of 1,235 inmates in 1948. The name was changed again in 1965, to Fairview Hospital and Training Center. Finally, in 1979, it was known simply as Fairview Training Center.

On February 24, 2000, the last resident left Fairview, ending a 92-year period of attempted altruism, medical treatment, and social experiments that, unfortunately, also included isolation of children who should have remained with their families. Treatment also included physical and emotional abuse, forced sterilizations, "time out" in cages, ice baths, and the liberal use of straitjackets, handcuffs, forced feedings, leg shackles, and psychotropic drugs. It's no wonder that numerous escape attempts occurred and an untold number of children and young adults died here. The official list of inmates who died at Fairview is short compared to the number of patients who simply disappeared from the roster of residents. It is known that, in 1970, two boys drowned in a small lake used by Fairview inmates for swimming and fishing. A cemetery once existed on the grounds, but some historians believe that several unofficial burial sites were filled between 1920 and 1950.

After Fairview's closure, a few former residents and staff members gave interviews to newspapers and TV news outlets or posted reports on the Internet about strange events they experienced in the residential units, common rooms, and the maze of underground tunnels that connect several buildings. Many of those reports suggested that the center was a site of intense paranormal activity.

Despite their mental incapacitation, it is likely that many residents were horrified to find themselves incarcerated there. Furthermore, many of them probably missed their families. It might be anticipated that, after death, residents would wait at

Fairview for the day when a mother or father would arrive to take them home. Other spirits, having been given up during their lifetimes by their parents, might remain there because they feel they have nowhere to go. Still others may be angry about forced sterilizations or other physical abuse and are waiting for revenge on doctors and staff members.

Hollie Pollock may continue to haunt the cistern near Fairview's Wythcombe Cottage because he is deeply distraught over the mutilation of his body. In November of 1923, Hollie was not present when roll call was taken. It was immediately assumed he had escaped from the facility, since such attempts were common. A few weeks later, pieces of skin and hair emerged from water pipes as staff members filled tubs for washing clothes. Someone suspected contamination of the cistern by a dead animal. When it was opened, the remains of Hollie's body were found. The paranormal activity at the site is said to be so intense that cars parked close by often fail to start. Others claim to hear a voice calling out from the now-covered cistern.

A Fairview doctor recounted his experience with a resident who suffered an epileptic seizure. At the time, the resident was alone, but he was quickly discovered by a woman who rushed to the adjacent building and alerted medical staff. After the patient was stabilized, questions were asked about the woman who had, in effect, saved the boy's life. No one came forward who could identify her. Days later, a photograph was found at the patient's bedside of his mother, who had died years earlier. The doctor was astonished when he realized that the person who had alerted staff to the medical emergency was the boy's dead mother.

After the training center closed, a team of security guards was employed to patrol the property all night, ensuring that vagrants and vandals did not enter the grounds. Several guards have reported seeing people, at a distance, wandering the grounds at night, yet on closer inspection, no one could be found. The figure most often sighted was that of a woman walking near the center's cottages.

Several people fortunate enough to get into Fairview after its closure have experienced screams, sobs, voices crying out

*Fairview Hospital and Training Center is now closed and slated for redevelopment, but many of its derelict buildings harbor the ghosts of inmates and staff who died there under miserable conditions.*

for help, and even growls. Some fascinating EVP have been captured here that may be accessed online.

A few years after Fairview's closure, a development group known as Sustainable Fairview Associates purchased 275 acres and several buildings. In 2004, the Pringle Creek Community was developed on 32 acres. So far, I have not discovered any reports of paranormal activity in the buildings that comprise this development. I would not be surprised if something strange occurs that residents simply don't feel inclined to reveal.

Go to Flickr.com and search for "Fairview Training Center." This site contains more than 800 photographs and a fascinating history. Also, on YouTube, you can view some amazing stories about Fairview residents who returned to the place many years after their departure.

## GHOST OF THE CIVIL WAR VETERAN

Thompson Brewery and Public House
3575 Liberty Road South
Salem 97302
503-363-7286
www.mcmenamins.com/thompson-brewery-public-house

Constructed in 1905 as a residence for Franklin (1841-1923) and Maria Thompson, this home has been transformed into a popular brewpub. Despite the modern equipment for producing and serving a vast array of drinks and food, the homey atmosphere of an early-20th-century house has been preserved. Old photographs of the town, a portrait of Franklin and Maria, low-angled ceilings on the second floor, and small rooms remind us that this place was once a dream home for a veteran of the Civil War who, on the day he moved in, was 63 years old. We can be certain that Franklin loved the house because it was built by his son, Fred Thompson, on 20 acres of lush pasture that fronted the market road to Eugene. Furthermore, when Franklin and Maria arrived in Salem at the invitation of their son, after they suffered through 40 years of frigid Minnesota winters, they surely found it to be a veritable paradise. It's no wonder, therefore, that Franklin's spirit remains in the house, usually in the second-floor room in which he died on November 23, 1923. Many staff members and astonished patrons have seen the apparition of a short man with gray hair at several locations within the house and at the rear of the building near the brewing facility.

A photograph of Franklin taken in 1907 may be viewed online. At that time, his hair was dark, yet thin, with a receding hairline. Sixteen years later, at the time of his death, it is likely that his hair was gray and quite thin. The bedroom where he died is located at the front of the house, on the north side. Today, it contains three tables and chairs for private parties. Franklin appears in this space, on the stairs leading down to the first floor, and near the front door. At times, he appears

*The Thompson Brewery and Public House is haunted by Civil War veteran Franklin Thompson, who died in a second-floor room.*

to be completely lifelike, and busy staff members rush by him thinking he is a customer. When they are struck by something odd about the man, they turn to find he has vanished.

A staff member told me that strange fragrances, including coffee, are often detected in many places within the house. In the kitchen, coffee beans are sometimes found spilled on the floor, suggesting Franklin loved coffee. In his former bedroom, disembodied voices and loud banging are heard, and condiments move on the tables. In some areas in the brewery and the old house, paranormal activity is so intense at times that staff members working late at night insist on staying close to each other.

It has been suggested that Mrs. Thompson also haunts the place. Known as a jokester, she is believed to move kitchen utensils, generate unexplained odors, and create loud bangs.

## GHOSTS OF THE PIONEERS

Salem Pioneer Cemetery
Hoyt at Commercial Street South
Salem 97302
503-588-6336
www.salempioneercemetery.org

Salem Pioneer Cemetery sits on a busy street, suggesting that daytime visits would be unlikely opportunities to experience anything paranormal. On a cold, dark day when the fog rolls in, however, this place, filled with looming monuments and massive trees, can be strangely quiet and quite freaky. As visitors move away from the Commercial Street side of the cemetery into the grove of madrones and oaks, older graves are found and an eerie atmosphere charges the air.

In 1853, the land now occupied by the center of this cemetery was the homestead of Rev. David Leslie and his second wife, Adelia. He established the first grave here when he buried his first wife, Mary A. Kinney Leslie, in 1841. Leslie added the graves of two daughters in 1854. That year, when the Independent Order of Odd Fellows purchased adjoining land for community burials, he sold his land, making this elevated spot, overlooking Salem, the town's foremost graveyard.

Among the notables in the graveyard are Asahel and Eugenia Bush (cemetery plot 66). Bush built the mansion that stands on Mission Street NE (see "Bush House," later in this chapter). William Graves is also buried in this graveyard, and that seems altogether fitting since he was a well-known and successful undertaker and gravedigger. Unfortunately, the location of his grave has been lost. Perhaps this is the reason why his ghost walks the cemetery at night. Ninety-six Civil War veterans are interred here, including three sailors who served in the Union Navy. In plot 44, you will find Tabitha Moffat Brown (1780-1858), one of the earliest pioneers to travel the Oregon Trail. A founder of Tualatin Academy, which later became Pacific University, she was dubbed the Mother of Oregon by the state legislature. Nearby, in plot 106, is Charles H. Bennett (1811-55). In 1848, he stood near John Marshall in the American River mill trace at the moment gold was discovered in California. He later served in the U.S. Army as captain of a cavalry unit and died in the Indian Wars.

Few cemeteries have active ghosts, but this graveyard is regarded as a great place to experience spirits. Since 2002, when a paranormal group encountered an incensed spirit that issued warnings to leave, several investigators have visited. They often seek an angry spirit that calls out to astonished visitors from an elevated place behind a tall monument. Some ghost hunters claim they have calmed this spirit and received his permission to continue touring the cemetery. During my investigations here, I got the impression this ghost is Graves. He may be frustrated rather than angry because the location of his grave has been lost. A colleague has suggested that the angry ghost may be Reverend Leslie.

At several locations, ghost hunters hear unexplained noises, such as a clanging sound that seems to emanate from a crypt. Audio recordings have captured footsteps, a baby crying, sobbing, a high-pitched male voice that says, "Hey, hey," and the sound of a violin.

## GHOSTS OF THE SIBLINGS

Bush House Museum
600 Mission Street NE
Salem 97302
503 363-1714
www.bushhousemuseum.org

The magnificent Bush House, which sits on a hill in Salem's

beautiful Bush's Pasture Park, gives us a glimpse of life and death more than a century ago. Today, the mansion is surrounded by a rose garden and wooded park bordered by busy streets. In the late 19th century, it stood in the center of a large tract of land as a symbol of the pioneer spirit, hard work, and great wealth that comes to those who are willing to take a chance. The Italianate Victorian mansion was constructed in 1877-78 by Asahel Bush II (1824-1913), who had gained his wealth by establishing a newspaper in 1851, winning election to the office of state printer in 1859, becoming a powerful political figure in Oregon, and operating one of the most successful banks in the Pacific Northwest. The 12-room house had every modern convenience money could buy, including indoor plumbing, central heating, gaslights, 10 fireplaces with Italian marble surrounds, and running water in each bedroom.

The happy day on which Bush moved into the estate was marred only by the fact that his wife, Eugenia, was not with him and their children, Asahel III (1858-1953), Estelle (1856-1942), Sally (1860-1946), and Eugenia (1862-1932). She had died 14 years earlier of tuberculosis. Despite that loss, the children grew up happy, well adjusted, and seemingly well prepared for the rigors of a university education. After high school, all of them left Salem for eastern universities and graduated, except Eugenia.

Apparently, the stress of life at a university in Massachusetts was too much for Eugenia and, in 1880 at the age of 18, she developed a mental illness diagnosed as schizophrenia. Urban legend says that her father moved her home to Salem and kept her confined in the basement. Historians dispute this claim and point out that wealthy Asahel II could afford the finest care available. In fact, Eugenia was sent to a hospital in Boston, where she received many years of treatment. Despite excellent care and frequent visits from her siblings, she did not return to the mansion in Salem until 1913, at the age of 51.

Biographers indicate that Sally and Eugenia had a special bond. Apparently, Asahel II preferred to keep Eugenia confined in a Boston hospital rather than endure the unpredictable and occasionally frightening behavior of a schizophrenic.

Immediately after his death, Sally boarded the family's private railroad car and sped to Boston, where she retrieved her beloved sister and transported her home to Salem. The haste with which this dramatic event took place suggests that Sally had been forbidden to bring Eugenia home while Asahel II was alive. Under the constant care of a live-in nurse and Sally's watchful eye, Eugenia resided in the house until her death in 1932. After decades in a mental hospital, Eugenia must have been so thrilled to be home with her sister, in beautiful Salem, that even death could not take her from this cherished place. The bond between these sisters may be the basis for some of the paranormal activity that occurs in the house.

During the 19 years preceding Eugenia's death, Sally managed the household and acted as a hostess for social affairs. Well known in Salem as Aunt Sally, she was generous to vagrants who begged for a meal at the kitchen door and a benevolent keeper of 27 cats and a beloved cow. After her death in 1946, her brother, Asahel III, moved back into the mansion at the age of 90 and remained there until he died in 1953.

Long lives spent in a grand mansion, animosity between father and daughter, a strong bond between two sisters, and a number of unavoidable yet tragic deaths have all contributed to a ghostly atmosphere within the Bush House. Original furnishings, selected by Sally Bush, add to the beautifully creepy ambience that visitors experience as they tour the place, yet staff members either deny knowledge of any paranormal phenomena or simply refuse to comment. Apparently, people associated with the current management don't want the place to become known as the proverbial haunted house. Many ghost hunters, however, believe that the building, now a museum, is haunted by the ghosts of Eugenia and her family.

Witnesses have spotted the apparition of a young woman as she descends the stairs and moves through several rooms on the main floor. Reportedly, this ghost plays with the thermostat controls. Several writers suggest that this ghost is Eugenia, who, after a 32-year stay in a mental hospital, has discovered a modern device that can make her home warmer.

It is possible, however, that this apparition is Sally and that she roams the house as mistress of the place, checking on the work of the servants and proper setting of the thermostat. Ghost hunters who visit the mansion should use an audio recorder to elicit a response from both Sally and Eugenia. Call out to "Aunt Sally" to prompt some fascinating EVP.

Upon the death of her husband in 1923, sister Estelle returned to live in the mansion. Her ghost may reside in one of the upstairs bedrooms and the parlor. She was known as an "elegant lady," and the swishing sound of a lady's long gown often heard in the parlor may signal Estelle's presence.

*Once the home of one of the region's wealthiest families, the Bush House is haunted by sisters Eugenia and Sally.*

## GHOSTS OF THE BALLROOM DANCERS

Reed Opera House
189 Liberty Street NE
Salem 97301
503-884-4614
www.thereedsalem.com

It is rare for two people to experience a paranormal phenomenon simultaneously, but that is exactly what happened when my son and I entered the third floor of this venerable old building. As soon as we stepped off the elevator, it was apparent that the atmosphere was different from that of the first and second floors. As we moved about the large ballroom, we agreed that the air seemed less dense, or lighter. We also felt as though we were walking 12 inches off the floor, on a surface that supported our weight but seemed soft.

Today, the Reed Opera House stands in downtown Salem as a reminder of the city's earliest commercial development. Still a popular social and business venue, the tall brick building is only a few blocks from the State Capitol. Built by Gen. Cyrus A. Reed (1825-1910), adjutant general of Oregon during the Civil War, the grand opera house opened on September 27, 1870, for the inaugural ball of Gov. LaFayette Grover. A few days later, numerous gas lanterns were lit to illuminate the stage for the first dramatic performance, *Frances Carroll, a Picture of State Life*. Many traveling theatre groups performed here over the next 30 years. Among the famous orators who attracted large audiences were Mark Twain, Susan B. Anthony, and Presidents Rutherford B. Hayes and Benjamin Harrison. Other events included the Firemen's Annual New Year's Ball, gubernatorial inaugurations, political meetings, and community celebrations.

In addition to hosting these occasions, the building included a large hotel and a saloon that, in 1893, was hailed as the best in town. It was also the busiest gambling venue the city has ever known.

By 1900, the opera house faced competition from more

modern and comfortable facilities, including the Grand Theater a few blocks away and the Chemeketa House. Dwindling audiences forced the owners to renovate the building into stores and offices. A major tenant, Miller's Department Store, remained in the building until 1970, when the place was sold. In 1975, new owners renovated it once again, creating the current configuration of shops and offices on the first and second floors and a huge ballroom on the third floor.

My review of the history of this grand old building did not uncover specific events that may have produced ghosts. In the saloon that once operated busy gambling tables, fights must have occurred, possibly leading to a fatality. In the hotel, an unfortunate traveler may have died, far from home, and lay in his room for a day or two before discovery. It was my impression, however, that the paranormal phenomena on the third floor include both imprints and ghosts.

*The Reed Opera House opened in 1870 as the city's premier entertainment venue. Today, it is a multi-use building that harbors ghosts on each floor.*

The atmospheric anomalies are likely created by intense imprints that seem to fill the entire floor. These may be residuals from great events staged there, such as Grover's inaugural ball. The minerals in the thick brick walls may have created the right electromagnetic conditions to retain these imprints and, perhaps, even amplify them. The ghosts that seemed to swirl around the room in a counterclockwise fashion gave me the impression that they were happy and enjoying one of the greatest events of their lives. This gathering may be composed of people who died at various places in Salem but returned to the opera house to continue the dance that gave them so much joy.

## GHOST OF THE ENTREPRENEUR

Elsinore Theatre
170 High Street SE
Salem 97301
503-375-3574
www.elsinoretheatre.com

Old theatres that presented live performances are among the top-five places to find ghosts. That's because musical performances, dramatic plays, and even comedy evoke so much passion from singers, musicians, and actors that a bond is created with the site that transcends death. Performers relish the adoration of audiences and, in many cases, the brilliance of their own accomplishments, so much that they cannot let go of that shining moment.

Audiences also contribute to the ghostly populations of old theatres. Captured by a sweet voice or powerful dramatic delivery, avid theatregoers sometimes fall in love with a favorite singer or actor. Attending performances night after night, they choose to remain in their reserved seats long after death, awaiting another chance to play out a one-sided love affair. Stagehands sometimes fall into this emotional chasm as well, but their passion for the theatre is most often directed at the machinery, lighting, elegant curtains, and stage props that they installed, maintained, and operated for many years. Falling from a high catwalk or succumbing to a heart attack while moving heavy backdrops, stagehands find themselves still on the job after death, caring for the one thing that made them a vital part of the theatre experience while they were alive.

Directors, producers, and theatre owners are often among the ghosts of old theatres because they are unwilling or unable to let go of the magnetic emotions of the creative process or lucrative business that made them famous and adored by their community. The man who built the Elsinore Theatre in downtown Salem, successful attorney George B. Guthrie (1882-1957), was so deeply passionate about his glorious accomplishment that he decided to stay on the scene to guide it through a number of troubled times and essential renovations, despite his death.

When the Elsinore Theatre opened on May 28, 1926, it was declared to be "the most beautiful theater in America" and "inspiring in aesthetic beauty." Designed to resemble the castle in the city of Elsinore in Shakespeare's *Hamlet*, its Tudor-Gothic architecture includes Povey Brothers stained-glass windows, 30-foot faux stonework walls, chandeliers, a decorative foyer, murals of Shakespeare's characters, and two grand carpeted staircases. The auditorium now seats 1,300 before a 30-by-60-foot stage framed by a decorative proscenium arch. Initially a venue for live performances by notables such as ventriloquist Edgar Bergen and Charlie McCarthy, Otis Skinner, Clark Gable, and the John Phillip Sousa Marine Band, the theatre also presented silent films, accompanied by music from a Wurlitzer organ in 1929. For the next 22 years, it continued to operate as a movie theatre, in addition to holding twice-weekly auditions by aspiring performers, including Doc Severinsen, who went on to fame on the Johnny Carson TV show. At times, the old theatre faced the possibility of demolition, but concerned citizens, and perhaps, the benevolent spirit of George Guthrie, saved the place. A series of ownership changes and multiple periods of renovation that ended in 2004 brought new life to this magnificent theatre.

Many people have spotted a wispy apparition, believed to be

George Guthrie, walk through several rows of seats. It seems likely that the seats now occupy a space that was originally an aisle, and Guthrie simply follows a familiar route. Some witnesses claim he appears with two young actresses on his arms. Maintenance-staff members often hear disembodied voices rise from the stage, as if invisible actors are rehearsing their scenes. Sound bursts of music, including notes from the old Wurlitzer organ, are frequently heard at night, when only a few staff members are present. Members of the audience, while waiting for a performance to begin, sometimes feel unseen beings pass close by as if ghosts are moving to their favorite seats.

As with most haunted theatres, isolated cold spots may be found onstage and in the wings. At times, staff members feel an unseen being rushing by between the stage and dressing rooms. Ghostly workers have been spotted on the backstage scaffolding dislodging dust that falls to the stage.

The best way to experience the Elsinore Theatre and its spirits is to attend an event. Today, the theatre offers a range of entertainment, from a Queen cover band to ballet and standup comedy. A tour of the theatre may be booked by calling 503-375-3574.

## GHOSTS OF THE OLD PLACES

Willamette Heritage Center
1313 Mill Street SE
Salem 97301
503-585-7012
www.willametteheritage.org

It is unfortunate that many cities in the U.S. have demolished hundreds of 19th-century homes and buildings that once housed historic businesses, laboratories, hospitals, courts, newspapers, and government offices in order to make room for freeways, malls, and stadiums. Places of worship, graveyards, and battlegrounds have been targeted by redevelopment agencies and dismantled or paved over to provide space for parking lots, factories, and office buildings. In my hometown, Alameda, California, many Victorian mansions built before 1880 were razed and replaced with small apartment buildings before anyone in government realized they had sanctioned the destruction of the town's history and cultural heritage. Before all was lost, some cities had the wisdom to establish heritage parks, where old buildings were moved, placed on sturdy foundations, renovated, and reopened as museums or rented as offices, meeting halls, retail space, or private residences. Oakland, California, established its famous Preservation Park, which contains 16 19th-century mansions gathered from various sites throughout the city and reopened as a dazzling upscale Victorian neighborhood that fascinates history buffs and ghost hunters. Salem created a similar venue at its Willamette Heritage Center. On this five-acre campus surrounding the 1895-vintage Thomas Kay Woolen Mill, nine historic structures comprise a priceless museum depicting the life and development of the community.

*Pleasant Grove Church:* Built in 1858 near Aumsville, Oregon, this historic church was moved to its current location in 1984. It is believed to be the oldest remaining Presbyterian church in the state. Some historians refer to it as the "Condit Church" because it was founded by Rev. Phillip Condit (1801-56), who arrived in Oregon in 1854. Although construction started only two years after his arrival, the church did not open its doors until April of 1858. Sound bursts of a male voice preaching the gospel have been heard by astonished visitors standing just inside the vacant church. Some ghost hunters speculate that these are paranormal manifestations of Reverend Condit, but history indicates that he never preached there. He died November 21, 1856, and is buried in Pleasant Grove Cemetery.

Condit's church remained in use for 86 years before falling into disrepair. For a few years, the building was completely neglected and nearly destroyed by squatters and vandals. Restoration began in the 1940s, preserving a remarkable building constructed of hand-hewn logs held together by wooden pegs, as well as its pews, pulpit, and stove.

This old church is haunted, but the identity of the spirit is unclear. It is possible that Reverend Condit has located the church he envisioned and is conducting the services he intended to perform before death put an end to his plans. His sons, Sylvanus and Cyrenius, who were instrumental in the fundraising and construction, may haunt the place, looking after a beloved house of worship that they literally carved out of the wilderness. Condit's colleague, Rev. J. A. Hanna, may be at the pulpit as well. After founding a church in Corvallis, he assisted in founding the Pleasant Grove Church by contributing his first year's salary to construction costs.

A strange light, often described as the flame of a candle, has been seen drifting across the church in front of the pulpit. Unexplained sounds include a violin, voices raised in song, boots tapping on the floor, and rattling of metal on the stove, as if an unseen hand were opening and then closing the tiny door to add wood to the fire.

***Jason Lee House:*** Built in 1841 on the site of the woolen mill's current water tower, the Lee house has a reputation as a haunted locale. It is a fascinating place, but I did not find it to be active in a paranormal sense. The rooms of both floors are filled with display boards depicting the history of the region, including Native American culture, wildlife, and Yankee pioneers. As a result, the house does not possess a mid-19th-century atmosphere. Ghosts may have attached themselves to some of the artifacts on display, but I did not get the impression that active spirits occupy the place. Other ghost hunters may have better luck finding ghosts in this house than I did. I interviewed people who had some compelling experiences on the stairs and in one of the second-floor rooms.

It is doubtful that Jason Lee's spirit occupies this house. In 1834, the evangelist led a group of Methodists from Missouri to Oregon to create a mission where local Indians would study the Bible. Arriving at a spot 13 miles north of present-day Salem, the group was plagued by floods and disease. Their relocation in 1841 to a spot called Chemeketa (a Native American word for "meeting" or "resting place") proved beneficial, as the missionaries built a gristmill, sawmill, and several buildings that would become the nucleus of Salem. A few years later, while visiting family in the East, Lee became ill. Recognizing the possibility that he might not recover, he made the arduous trip to his family home in Stanstead, Canada, and died there March 12, 1845, at the age of 41.

The families of Lewis Judson, Josiah Parrish, and W. W. Raymond also resided in this house over the years. EVP sweeps that invite these people to speak may be productive.

***John D. Boon House:*** This may be the most haunted house at Willamette Heritage Center. With the exception of one room, this little building is a faithful representation of a family home from the 1840s. Believed to be the oldest single-family dwelling still standing in Salem, the place contains a kitchen, parlor, dining room, and bedroom, with period furnishings that include a cast-iron stove and organ. Built in 1847, it was home to the John D. Boon family. Boon (1817-64) arrived in the region in 1845 and achieved quick success in the lumber and wool industries. As a well-established leader in business and society, he became treasurer of Oregon Territory in 1851 and, in 1859, of the State of Oregon, serving until 1862. He constructed a brick building in 1860, still standing at 888 Liberty Street NE, for use as State Treasury offices. Today, it houses the popular McMenamin's brewpub known as Boon's Treasury.

John D. Boon died in Salem on July 17, 1864, at the age of 47. He is buried in Salem Pioneer Cemetery, but I suspect that his ghost still resides in his house. The bedroom has been converted to a media room with a few benches and a screen mounted on a wall. This modern intrusion has apparently aroused a spirit who does not like the alteration. When my son entered the room, he was immediately pushed backward by unseen hands. Upon crossing the threshold, he also felt an abrupt change in the atmosphere. After listening to his report, I attempted to enter the room but encountered a wall of energy a few inches inside the doorway. Moving ahead, I felt large hands push against my shoulders. Clearly recognizing a malevolent spirit or, at least, one that did not like a paranormal investigator intruding on its space, I decided to leave the house.

***Methodist Parsonage:*** The Parsonage was built in 1841 under the supervision of Jason Lee and Gustavus Hines with lumber produced by the Methodist mission's sawmill. Originally designed as a duplex to house the families of two missionaries, part of the building was eventually used as the Indian Manual Labor School while a schoolhouse was under construction. The place originally stood at 1325 Ferry Street but was sold in the late 1840s, as the Methodist mission was disbanded. The building served as a boardinghouse for many years until falling into disrepair. Eventually, the house was moved to the heritage center, restored, and filled with artifacts from the Methodist mission period.

A docent told me that strange sounds are often heard in this house when no tourists or other staff members are present. These sounds include muted whispers, soft footsteps as though an unseen person walked about in bare feet or slippers, and doors opening and closing.

Aside from Jason Lee and his family, others who lived in the home with large families include the Reverends Gustavus Hines and Hamilton Campbell. Members of their families and numerous short-term residents may have loved the comfortable house so much that they remain there long after death.

***Murder Bridge:*** The ghostly image of a woman has been seen running across the bridge that spans Mill Creek adjacent to the dye house. Those who have observed this spirit claim she has a crazed expression on her face as though she is in fear of losing her life. A few people have reported that they spotted the woman's husband chasing after her. Both ghosts disappear as they complete their crossing. Some accounts state that in the early 20th century, a man murdered his wife on this bridge. Both were employed at the woolen mill, and the husband suspected that the wife had become infatuated with a man who worked in the dye house. I was unable to verify any of these claims, but I did speak to a docent and two locals who report having seen the frightened woman. A review of available newspaper and police records spanning 1900 to 1920 failed to reveal any information about a murder on this bridge. It is possible that a murder occurred here long before the mill and bridge were constructed in 1896 and the ghostly couple plays out their tragic event on the modern structure. It is interesting to note that the brick mill that stands today replaced an earlier structure that burned in 1889. The ghosts of a crazed woman and angry man spotted dashing across the bridge may be linked somehow to the historic fire rather than a lover's triangle that ended in murder.

***Thomas Kay Woolen Mill:*** Among the defining elements of the 19th-century industrial revolution, with its large factories, were six-day workweeks, with a shift spanning 12 hours, and fatal injuries of unprotected workers caused by noisy, fast-moving machines. A tour of this fascinating wool mill reveals numerous machines that likely led to severe injury or death for workers who were sometimes as young as eight years old. After dying in this crowded, noisy place, spirits certainly would want to move on to some peaceful, cherished house or farm, but some may be trapped here, afraid to leave a job that saved their family from misery and starvation.

Today, visitors who tour this 1895-vintage mill find it quiet, yet there are ghosts around still at work. On the second floor, at the wool carding machines, a transparent figure sometimes appears with a dazed expression on his face. His legs are not visible, but his fingers look stretched and bloodied. On the first floor, the ghostly image of a man wearing a black vest, white shirt, and string necktie walks from one end of the building to the other, apparently overseeing invisible workers.

At times, astonished visitors hear the sounds of machinery start up or drive shafts overhead begin to turn. These sounds are brief and may be mistaken for those generated by trucks outside the building.

In the turbine room, adjacent to the mill, an angry spirit manifests in several ways, ranging from dark energy, perceived by sensitive people, to sharp screams in a masculine voice. It has been reported that a worker was killed by the water-driven turbine while attempting to perform maintenance on the device.

***Wayne the Groundskeeper:*** Many reports on the Internet mention a groundskeeper named Wayne who haunts several locations at the heritage center. Wayne Mentzer worked in the mill's machine shop until his retirement in 1968. He loved the place so much that he stayed on as a volunteer groundskeeper until his death in 1984 at the age of 79. Apparently, death

*The restored Thomas Kay Woolen Mill allows visitors to step back in time, to 1895, and experience the ghosts who labored 12 hours per day and died here.*

hasn't stopped Wayne from going to work at the mill. His ghost has been spotted in the machine shop he loved so much and at various sites around the park. It has been reported that he used to leave food out for the mice. Ghost hunters might attract his attention and capture his voice on EVP recordings if this fact were mentioned.

## THE SALEM HANGING TREE

Church Street at D Street NE
Salem 97301

The intersection of Church and D Streets marks a place that

was well known as Salem's hanging ground from about 1854 to 1866. Previous to the selection of this spot for public executions, the first hanging in Salem was staged on ground now occupied by a covered parking lot for the SAIF Building (the state-chartered workers'-compensation insurance company) at 400 High Street SE. At that site, murderer William Kendall was dispatched to the great beyond on April 18, 1851, for killing William Hamilton over a land-use dispute. Kendall's trial and execution were swift, because the town had no jail or other secure facility for keeping prisoners. Recognizing the problem, the County Board of Commissioners contracted for the construction of a jail on lower Church Street near Mill Creek. A nearby tree was used as a gallows for several hangings at this site until 1866, when the Oregon State Penitentiary was transferred from Portland to Salem. The new facility conducted executions by hanging and firing squad, but the general public was not permitted to witness these events.

The number of hangings that occurred on Church Street is uncertain, but two of them endure as local legends. Charles I. Rose has the distinction of being the first man executed after Oregon attained statehood. His guilt for the murder of his second wife, Angelica Carpenter, was easily established, as he confessed to the killing and two witnesses corroborated his admission.

A hanging staged in 1865 became entrenched in history because two murderers were executed simultaneously. On the night of January 9, 1865, saloonkeeper George Beale and his friend, butcher George Baker, approached the home of Daniel Delaney with the intention of robbing him of a large amount of money rumored to be stashed there. As Delaney resisted, the two shot him and fired at a boy who worked in the house. A speedy trial rendered a guilty verdict and May 17 was set as the execution day. Owing to Delaney's popularity and the unique double hanging, more than a thousand people crowded around the hanging tree at the corner of Church and D Streets, eager for a view of the event.

Today, tall trees stand at the edge of Mill Creek, very close to the intersection of Church and D Streets. Local ghost hunters believe that one of those trees served as the gallows for Beale, Baker, and Rose, largely because paranormal phenomena have been detected among them. Strange things do occur at this spot, but I doubt that a hanging tree stands amid the current grove of trees. A historical account published by Ben Maxwell in 1945 indicates that the court paid the Wilbur brothers to construct a scaffold and gallows, suitable for a double hanging, in a grove of small trees at the southeast corner of Church and Mill (later D Street) Streets. Aside from that, an arborist told me that the trees that currently stand at the edge of Mill Creek are not old enough to have been of sufficient size and strength for a hanging in 1865.

APPENDIX A

# Suggested Reading

## BOOKS


Allison, Ross, and Joe Temples. *Ghostology 101: Becoming a Ghost Hunter.* Seattle: AuthorHouse, 2005.

Auerbach, Loyd. *ESP, Hauntings, and Poltergeists.* New York: Warner Books, 1986.

———. *Ghost Hunting: How to Investigate the Paranormal.* **Oakland: Ronin Publishing, 2004.**

———. *A Paranormal Casebook: Ghost Hunting in the New Millennium.* **Dallas: Atriad Press, 2005.**

Brown, Sylvia. *Adventures of a Psychic.* New York: Penguin Books, 1990.

Cobb, Todd. *Ghosts of Portland.* Atglen, PA: Schiffer Publishing, 2007.

Davis, Jefferson. *Haunted Astoria.* Portland: Norseman Ventures, 2006.

Dwyer, Jeff. *The Art and Science of Paranormal Investigation.* CreateSpace, 2012.

———. *Ghost Hunter's Guide to California's Gold Rush Country.* Gretna, LA: Pelican Publishing, 2009.

———. *Ghost Hunter's Guide to California's Wine Country.* Gretna, LA: Pelican Publishing, 2008.

———. *Ghost Hunter's Guide to Monterey and California's Central Coast.* Gretna, LA: Pelican Publishing, 2010.

———. *Ghost Hunter's Guide to Los Angeles.* Gretna, LA: Pelican Publishing, 2007.

———. *Ghost Hunter's Guide to New Orleans: Revised Edition.* Gretna, LA: Pelican Publishing, 2016.

———. *Ghost Hunter's Guide to Portland and the Oregon Coast.* Gretna, LA: Pelican Publishing, 2015.

———. *Ghost Hunter's Guide to Seattle and Puget Sound.* Gretna, LA: Pelican Publishing, 2008.

———. *Ghost Hunter's Guide to the San Francisco Bay Area: Revised Edition.* Gretna, LA: Pelican Publishing, 2011.

———. *Psychic: Use Your Psychic Power to Experience Ghosts.* CreateSpace, 2013.

Eufrasio, Al, and Jeff Davis. *Weird Oregon.* New York: Sterling Publishing, 2010.

Groff, Nick, and Jeff Belanger. *Chasing Spirits: The Building of the* Ghost Adventures *Crew.* New York: New American Library, 2012.

Hauck, Dennis William. *Haunted Places: The National Directory.* New York: Penguin Group, 2002.

Hawes, Jason, Grant Wilson, and Michael Jan Friedman. *Ghost Hunting: True Stories of Unexplained Phenomena from the Atlantic Paranormal Society.* New York: Pocket Publishers, 2007.

Holzer, Hans. *Ghosts I've Met.* Chicago: Barnes and Noble Books, 2005.

———. *True Ghost Stories.* Chicago: Barnes and Noble Books, 2001.

Schlosser, S. E., and Paul G. Hoffman. *Spooky Oregon: Tales of Hauntings, Strange Happenings, and Other Local Lore.* Guilford, CT: Globe Pequot, 2009.

Smitten, Susan. *Ghost Stories of Oregon.* Auburn, WA: Lone Pine Publishing, 2002.

Southall, R. H. *How to Be a Ghost Hunter.* Woodbury, MN: Llewellyn Publications, 2003.

Steiger, Brad. *Real Ghosts, Restless Spirits, and Haunted Places.* Detroit: Visible Ink Press, 2003

Taylor, Troy. *Ghost Hunter's Guidebook.* Alton, IL: White Chapel Productions Press, 1999.

———. *Ghost Hunter's Guidebook: The Essential Guide to Investigating Ghosts and Hauntings.* Alton, IL: White Chapel Productions, 2007.

———, Robert Wlodarski, and Anne Wlodarski. *Talking with the Dead.* Alton, IL: White Chapel Productions, 2009.

Van Praagh, James. *Ghosts Among Us: Uncovering the Truth about the Other Side.* New York: HarperOne, 2008.

Zwicker, Roxie. *Haunted Portland: From Pirates to Ghost Brides.* Charleston, SC: The History Press, 2007.

## ARTICLES

Adams, Anne. "Halloween Haunt Spots." *Portland Monthly Magazine,* 29 October 2010.

Anderson, Jennifer. "Stumptown Stumper." *Portland Tribune,* 30 October 2009.

Associated Press. "Ghost Buster: Ohio Woman inspires CBS' Supernatural Series." *Boston Herald,* 4 July 2005.

Baird, K. "Haunted Eugene." *Eugene Daily News,* 4 December 2013.

Bella, Rick. "Clackamas Town Center Shooter Carried 145 Rounds, Fired 17 Shots." *Oregonian,* 1 May 2013.

Boryczka, Elena. "A Haunted House." *Beaverton Valley Times,* 26 October 2006.

Clark, Jayne. "10 Great Places to Get Spooked by Your Surroundings." *USA Today*, 26 October 2007.

Giovannetti, Joe. "Crossing Over: Ghost Hunter Knows Things that Go Bump in the Night." *Fairfield (CA) Daily Republic*, 18 October 2007.

Hannah, James. "Who Ya Gonna Call for the Paranormal?" *San Francisco Chronicle*, 8 June 2008.

Harger, Steve. "Seeking Spirits." *New York Times*, 30 October 2009.

Irwin, Richard. "Jeff Dwyer's Ghost Stories Aren't Just for Halloween." *Long Beach Press Telegram*, 17 June 2007.

Jenkins, Chris, and Colin Fly. "Haunted Hotel Has Baseball Players Walking." *San Francisco Chronicle*, 26 July 2009.

Jensen, Evan. "Is There a Ghost in Estacada?" *Estacada News*, 1 October 2008.

King, Tim. "Ghosts and Haunted Places in Oregon and Beyond. " *Salem News*, 29 October 2007.

Kirby, Carrie. "Ghost Hunters Utilize Latest in Technology." *San Francisco Chronicle*, 31 October 2005.

Kurhi, Eric. "Investigating the Eerie Historic Hayward Mansions." *Oakland Tribune*, 13 December 2009.

Mirk, Sarah. "The Ghosts of Lone Fir Cemetery." *Portland Mercury*, 29 October 2009.

Moran, Gwen. "Real-Life Ghost Busters." *USA Weekend*, 31 October 2004.

Newell, Cliff. "Spooky Times for Ghost Hunters." *Portland Tribune*, 30 October 2008.

Perry, Douglas. "Portland's Real-Life Hauntings: 5 Ghost Sightings That Caused Panic, Earned Headlines." *Oregonian* (Portland, OR), 10 October 2018.

Pierleoni, Allen. "'Ghost Whisperer' Consultant Speaks Out." *Sacramento Bee*, 2 January 2008.

Ridgeway, Suzie. "Portland Haunted Tour." *Portland Tribune*, 27 October 2006.

Schoolmeester, Ron. "10 Great Places to Go on a Haunted Hike." *USA Today*, 28 July 2006.

Sichelman, Lew. "Plenty of Spooky Sites around the Nation." *San Francisco Chronicle*, 28 October 2007.

Wach, Bonnie. "The Dead Zone." *San Francisco Chronicle*, 31 October 2004.

## APPENDIX B

# Films, DVDs, and Videos

Fictional films may provide you with information that will assist you in preparing for a ghost hunt. This assistance ranges from putting you in the proper mood for ghost hunting to useful techniques for exploring haunted places. Some films, especially documentaries, provide information about the nature of ghostly activity.

*An American Haunting* (2006). Directed by Courtney Solomon, starring Donald Sutherland and Sissy Spacek.

*The Conjuring* (2013). Directed by James Wan, starring Vera Farmiga, Patrick Wilson, and Lili Taylor.

*Dragonfly* (2002). Directed by Tom Shadyac, starring Kevin Costner and Kathy Bates.

*The Fog* (2005). Directed by Rupert Wainwright, starring Tom Welling and Maggie Grace.

*1408* (2007). Directed by Mikael Hafstrom, starring John Cusack and Samuel L. Jackson.

*Haunted* (1995). Directed by Lewis Gilbert, starring Aidan Quinn and Kate Beckinsale.

*Haunting in Connecticut* (2009). Directed by Peter Cornwell, starring Virginia Madsen and Martin Donovan.

*The Haunting of Seacliff Inn* (1995). Directed by Walter Klenhard, starring Ally Sheedy and William R. Moses.

*Hereafter* (2010). Directed by Clint Eastwood, starring Matt Damon.

*Insidious* (2010). Directed by James Wan, starring Patrick Wilson and Rose Byrne.

*Living With the Dead* (2000). Directed by Stephen Gyllenhaal, starring Ted Danson and Mary Steenburgen.

*The Others* (2001). Directed by Alejandro Amenabar, starring Nicole Kidman.

*Paranormal Activity* (2009). Directed by Oren Peli, starring Katie Featherston.

*Paranormal Activity 2* (2010). Directed by Tod Williams, starring Katie Featherston.

*Paranormal Activity: The Marked Ones* (2014). Directed by Christopher Landon, starring Andrew Jacobs and Jorge Diaz.

*ParaNorman (2012)*. Directed by Chris Butler and Sam Fell, starring Kodi Smit-McPhee, Tucker Albrizzi, and Anna Kendrick. Animated.

*The Rite* (2011). Directed by Mikael Hafstrom, starring Anthony Hopkins and Colin O'Donoghue.

*Sightings: Heartland Ghost* (2002). Directed by Brian Trenchard-Smith, starring Randy Birch and Beau Bridges.

*The Sixth Sense* (1999). Directed by M. Night Shyamalan, starring Bruce Willis and Haley Joel Osment.

*Stir of Echoes* (1999). Directed by David Koepp, starring Kevin Bacon.

*Thir13en Ghosts* (2001). Directed by Steve Beck, starring Tony Shalhoub.

*White Noise* (2005). Directed by Geoffrey Sax, starring Michael Keaton.

The following movies are not about ghosts, but they are worth watching before visiting Portland and the Oregon coast. They provide a sneak preview of some of the scenery and a bit of local culture.

*Are We There Yet?* (2005). Filmed in the Pearl District, the Max Tunnel, and parts of central Portland.

*Cold Weather* (2011). A former forensic-science student investigates the mysterious disappearance of his ex-girlfriend.

*Gone* (2012). A woman is convinced that her kidnapper has returned when her sister goes missing. Filmed in the metropolitan Portland area.

*House of Last Things* (2013). Some scenes filmed at Hotel deLuxe on SW Fifteenth Avenue in Portland.

*Lean on Pete* (2017). A teenager gets a summer job working for a horse trainer and befriends the fading racehorse. Filmed at the former Portland Meadows racetrack.

*The Hunter* (2003). Many scenes were filmed in downtown Portland.

*Men of Honor* (2000). Scenes at a restaurant and other exterior shots were filmed in Portland.

*Ten Days in a Madhouse* (2015). Story of Nellie Bly's exposé of an insane asylum. Filmed in Salem.

*Untraceable* (2008). Set in Portland, a serial killer rigs contraptions that kill his victims.